GW01035609

When There Are Few Words

Exploring some of the questions that might arise for you, or someone close to you, at end of life

By Deirdre Mc Kenna

Published by Kirwin Maclean Associates

enquiries@kirwinmaclean.com

www.kirwinmaclean.com

First published in 2024
Kirwin Maclean Associates
43 Tamary Road
Mayobridge
Newry
BT34 2HW

Typesetting by Tora Kelly
Cover design by Tora Kelly
Cover image by Lisa Morrison
All images are copyright of Deirdre Mc Kenna unless stated
otherwise

Printed and bound in Great Britain by 4edge, Essex

ISBN - 978-1-912130-91-7
eISBN - 978-1-912130-90-0

For

Maisie and Frank

Contents

Foreword by Kelly McCartney

I have known Deirdre (Dee) for many years, first meeting in a professional capacity when we worked together within a community specialist palliative care team. While colleagues, we soon became firm friends and have remained so since.

Dee, a Sister of Mercy and a Social Worker embodies someone who puts their heart into all that they do. It would be accurate to say that I don't know anyone who so earnestly seeks to serve others. In her work within the field of palliative care, Dee is a champion not only for the person receiving care, but also for their loved ones or anyone who would seek to support them in this time of need. She is a voice oftentimes for those who need it most and a warm, kind presence always.

As a friend, Dee has helped me in understanding the upset and turmoil times such as these bring. I am so glad this help, and support, can now reach others through this book. There are so many questions that exist in a space of loss and anguish. Many heartbroken pieces that are hard to put back together. You may find yourself with a sense of overwhelm, of where even to begin. If you find yourself facing the tragedy of loss, please be assured that it is safe to read on. As you turn the pages of this book to seek answers, painful as your questioning may be, you will find the kindest guidance. You will also find swathes of compassion that recognises just how difficult and vulnerable this time is for you.

Dee's many years of experience, knowledge and skills inform this book, which offers you confidence in her capability in this area. Alongside this, you as a reader will also experience her nature. Dee is a woman of integrity, to meet her is to know this, and to witness her warm, joyous smile in all that she does. While you may feel there is little to smile about at present, you will, no doubt welcome the genuine warmth and companionship offered here.

Within the pages of this book, you will find hope in having some answers to your questions, in the prompts to support your conversations and in the relief of knowing you are not alone. Please be reassured, that in the midst of the pain and distress, there is a warm, comforting guide who will meet you where you are, and journey with you where you seek to go.

Kelly McCartney
(Health service employee with lived experience)

Introduction

Hello, and welcome to these pages. We pick up, or are gifted certain books, for many different reasons. Perhaps, for you, you are searching through these pages because you find yourself in one of the most difficult times in your life. Perhaps you find yourself, or someone close to you, facing serious illness, or approaching end of life. If this is how you have come to these pages, then I want to say to you, firstly, how sorry I am. I am sorry for the heartache you are likely feeling at this time. These are such hard times for you, and maybe you feel at a bit of a loss, in the midst of it all. At a loss about what to do, about what to say, or about how to say what you want to say. My heart goes out to you, and you are so very welcome here.

There may be others of you, who have perhaps come to these pages because you're curious. Curious about a book like this; curious about a book that considers end of life and explores some of the questions that may arise. You too are welcome, and maybe you will find an ease here, in thinking and talking, or wondering about, the subject of dying and death.

For some of you, perhaps this book has come to you, because you are trying to find ways to help others. Help others to find their way through the pain of having someone they love, or care for, someone important to them, who is very ill. Or maybe you are trying to help them manage when the end of life is near, to support them through their dying and death, or the dying and death of someone they care for.

However you have come to this book, you are welcome. You are welcome here, to take and sift through what is written. To find what is useful or helpful in this offering. To take away what is useful to you at this time and leave behind what doesn't feel right for you or fit your need.

It is my hope that there is something of value in these pages for you. Something that may help you find your way on this unknown, or unfamiliar path you now walk. That in these pages, there may be something that feels close to companionship. That something in these pages, offers you some comfort, or accompaniment, in these weeks and days and hours. A quiet, gentle guide to you, that you can pick up and set down again, as and when you feel so inclined.

For those of you seeking knowledge, may you find something that expands and broadens that which you already know. That, which you have already learned from your own experience. So welcome; welcome to this book and let us be companions, one to another, navigating these difficult times. When your heart is tender, and you feel unsure, may this book serve to whisper words to you, when there are few words.

Please be mindful of yourself, as you read or listen to these pages. Find a pace that works for you. The questions in this book may, in and of themselves, feel very sore or hard for you to read. They may raise in you some very painful feelings, of loss, of grief, of love or heartache, so it is important not to overwhelm yourself. Try to find a pace of reading, or listening to this book, that allows you pay attention to how your heart is coping. Each question can carry a world of emotion, and it is important that you go as gently as you can. Pick the book up and leave it down again, according to your pace or need. Take the time you need within the time you have available. Gently, gently now, let us step on together.

So, who am I?

I'm a sister of mercy and a social worker. I qualified as a social worker in 1990. Since 2008, I have specialised in palliative and end of life care. I spent seven years working as a social worker in a hospice before joining a community specialist palliative care team. In the community, I worked with people in their own homes, who had a palliative diagnosis. As a social worker, my work has always involved the person, close family members, carers, or those people important to the person. For people without family, those close to them could include friends or neighbours; people they trust and who they know well. For many years, in my work I have been with people who are very ill and people who are dying. It is from this experience, that I offer you some of what I have learned and have come to know.

My work has brought me into the homes and lives of people facing the reality of their own mortality, their own dying and end of life. People who had received the sad news that they had a palliative diagnosis, a diagnosis that they had an illness that could be treated but could not be cured. It's likely hard for you reading this, to begin to imagine what that must be like for someone; to hear such news. In my experience, it is always very hard, it comes as a shock, and it usually takes some time for people to actually take it in.

Alongside the busyness of clinical appointments, treatments, symptoms management, people often find themselves trying to explore important questions about the meaning and purpose of their lives. Find themselves having to begin thinking about and planning ahead for a very different future than the one they had imagined. Trying to manage some really strong emotions like fear, regret, anger, despair. Reflecting on the place of love, and hope, or faith in their lives.

Over these years, I have had many conversations with people about these really important things in life. Conversations that were spoken from the heart and were often very emotional. As you can imagine, this work often felt very privileged to me. Privileged that I was allowed into these people's lives at such a time; that I was allowed to either give witness to their reflections and explorations of their life's journey, or to support them find their way through.

So, why write this book?

I know the good level of support provided through palliative care services, particularly around care, support and treatment. I know the opportunities many people with a palliative diagnosis, have for conversations about their end of life care, their dying and death. I also know that many of us will live out our lives without ever coming in contact with specialist palliative care teams. For most of us, who live out our lives at home, or maybe in a care home, in our local community, we have much less, if any, contact with health and social care services, apart from with our GP.

For us then, and for those who care for us, we are less likely to have the opportunities to ask the sort of questions that this book addresses. And often, we don't even know we need to be asking any such questions at all. So, it may be harder for us to know what is happening as we move closer to end of life. We may not realise or recognise the nearness of our dying and death, or that of someone close to us.

I know too, from my own experience of going to wakes or funerals of neighbours and friends, that people can be taken completely by surprise when someone they loved or cared for, has come naturally to their end of life and has died. Where the person has been living at home, I have listened to family members describe their disbelief that the person has died. They can be shocked by the person's death, even where there may have been signs, that the person had been declining over time, was nearing their end of life, and would soon die. This can be very hard to deal with. It can also affect how someone grieves their loss, and lives through their bereavement.

So, I thought it might be useful to write this book for people in a similar situation. Those of you who, for example, have older family members living their lives at home, or in a care home. That this book might help you have some of the information you may need, some guidance that you can read, if and when you need it.

We are, of course, all different. And how we come to the end of our lives is different. It isn't exactly the same for all of us. For some of us, our health may decline over years or months, while for others our decline may come more suddenly, even over weeks or days. So, some of the information here may help your particular experience and circumstance, some other parts may not. I trust that you will sift and find what is helpful for you.

As I was writing, I was thinking you may be searching for information or guidance to a particular question, and that you might only read or listen to the response to that one. So, each of the questions can be read as a stand alone question, even though there are many connections between them all. As a consequence, if you do read more than one question, you may hear a few important things are repeated.

and so, let's begin...

Do we have to tell them?

Just below the surface of this question, lies a very real concern. The concern to shield the person, protect them from the sad news, is often keenly felt by the one who asks. They may harbour a fear that if the person is told or knows how ill they are, or that they may only have a short time to live, then they might lose hope or become overwhelmed by the information. This concern is very understandable, coming as it often does, from a place of care or love for the person.

Sometimes those close to the person, have been speaking with the doctor, and have been told that the person they love or care for is dying. Perhaps the person themselves though, has not had this conversation with the doctor, or may have chosen not to ask the doctor for such medical information.

You, or others close to the person, may feel it's best that the person doesn't know, because you fear that if they did know, they'd be too upset. You might also worry that they might just 'give up' on the living that remains to them. Out of kindness, you may be anxious to keep this information from the person and believe it's best not to tell them.

So let's think this through. We are all very different. Some of us like to have any information that's available; we like to know what we're dealing with, and this helps us plan, or make choices, about what to do next. Some of us prefer to wait and see what happens, adjusting our plans according to what is going on at the particular time. No one will force information on you or on those close to you.

What might happen instead, is that the doctor will ask you or those close to you, what you know already about how things are with your illness. Listening to how you answer, allows the doctor have a sense of your understanding of where things stand. They may then offer to sensitively provide you with a fuller picture, with their honest assessment of how you're doing medically.

The doctor will be alert to whether you or those close to you, want to hear such information or not. If someone says they don't want such information, then the doctor will not insist on telling them. Instead, they will likely reassure the person, that if some questions do come up later, then they can always ask. You are not expected to insist on telling someone either, if that person doesn't want to know.

If, however, the person asks the doctor, or asks you, then it is always important to answer honestly, painful as this may feel to you. Your honesty here is a mark of your respect for the person; respecting them enough to answer such a question honestly. When the doctor answers honestly, it shows they respect the person too and that the person has a right to know. The idea of having to have such a conversation with someone you love or care for, may feel a bit overwhelming, but don't worry, we will take some time in this book to look at it together.

Sometimes, even when the doctor has been asked for information, it may be hard for you or those close to you, to really make sense of what is being said. Sometimes the information has a lot of medical language that you may not understand. Sometimes too, the information is couched or phrased in such a way that we miss the meaning. When this happens, we can be left feeling unsure, unclear and uncertain. At worst, we might still be completely unaware of what we were actually told. This issue of communication is very important, so we will take some more time with it and look at it on its own, as a separate question in this book.

But first, back to the question you asked here about whether or not to tell the person. I have known times when the person themselves knew that they were dying but never mentioned it, never spoke of it. And the family members knew that the person was dying, and never spoke of it or mentioned it. Each one kept their counsel so as not to cause upset or pain to the other. Each afraid to say something for fear of causing upset or distress to the other. So, it was never spoken of aloud; each one carrying the burden of this information privately and quietly, with no conversation between the two. There may have been feelings of guilt about having information which the other person did not have. Maybe there are private worries about what the next few days or weeks or months will be like. Opening this conversation up, as emotional as it may be, allows for some sharing of these fears and worries. It allows some space for everyone to feel easier and freer around one another, to talk and laugh and cry together. It may provide some certainty to each one, in the midst of such uncertain times, that all who need to know, know. Choices and decisions can then be made in full knowledge.

Perhaps it will help to think of it in this way. There are two key moments in all of our lives. The first is the moment we are born and take our first breath. The second is the moment when we take our last breath, the moment we die. Then consider this: all the preparation, the conversations, the planning and so on, that goes into getting ready for that first moment, the moment we take our first breath as a newborn baby. Now think of how that compares, how little preparation or conversation or planning, we have in anticipation of, or readiness for, that second key moment, the moment we draw our last breath and die. When we think about the question in this light, perhaps we can see that telling the person truthfully, when they ask, or offering them opportunities to speak about their end of life and dying, could actually help by providing the person some time to prepare.

Having the information can allow the person time to speak to people they may wish to speak to; perhaps they want to make a will or talk about their wishes for their funeral. Sore as attending to these practical tasks may be, they can provide the person with great peace of mind and enable them work through these important tasks themselves. And for so many, having this awareness allows them to consider those core spiritual or existential questions that may arise around their life's meaning and purpose; faith, hope, regret, love, fear and forgiveness. This then provides the opportunity for them to speak to a chaplain, a priest or a spiritual guide with whom they are comfortable.

Thinking about your question in this context then, may help you come to see that honesty here is a great kindness you can offer to the one you love or care for, and could well contribute to that greater gift that helps a person die well.

You may feel worried now, that this all seems far too much. You may feel pressure that these conversations have to happen: that if they don't you have somehow let the person down. No, no this is not the case. The best that any of us can hope for, is that we are offered opportunities to say what we might like to say. Some people may take these gentle invitations and begin to talk, others may not. Some people don't feel the need to say anything at all, and that too is alright. So, do not put any pressure on yourself that you have to force a conversation, that people have to talk. You know this person best, and you will have some idea of what might be best here for them and you.

If you do feel that you would like to try to offer the person the opportunity to talk, a few suggestions might be useful to you. If the person has been struggling with, recurring infections, for example, or have had a few unplanned admissions to hospital, you could begin by simply saying something like, "these past few days/weeks/months, have been very hard for you, haven't they". Then wait for a moment to allow the person make whatever response they wish. The response they make will help guide you with what you might say next. So, for example, they might agree and say something like "I'm fed up with it all". Or, "I'm not going back into hospital". This allows you then to follow up with an enquiry about what they think they might want instead.

Another suggestion for a gentle way of offering an opportunity to talk, could be to begin by saying how you feel. "I've been worrying these last days/weeks/months about how you're doing and was thinking, maybe you feel a bit worried too?" Again, leave a short pause here to allow the person to respond. You can take your cue from them. Or, maybe you could simply say that you love them and reassure them of how much you care; and that too is more than enough. Have a think about what might feel alright for you, and, remember, there is no script here, there is no right or wrong. The relationship you have with the person and how you have expressed yourselves over the years, will help you find your way in this.

Quick reference: Do we have to tell them?

If the person does not want to know, we respect their wishes not to be told.

If the person wants to know, then it is good to tell them.

Keep checking with them for when they've had enough information.

Reassure them that if they think of other questions later, they can ask.

Offer opportunities to the person, to ask for information.

Take your lead from the person.

Reflection: Do we have to tell them?

How would it be to just be quiet now?
Allow the press and stress of speaking fall,
And in it's place, create a space that opens into softer
sounds,
The breathing in and breathing out
of kindred hearts.

How would it be to find a rhythm there,
That soothes and smoothes the irksome edge
of any burdened sense?
That gives release to musts and shoulds and loosens
tangled thoughts?

How might it be to let some words, from this first silent
place,
find gentle form, when speaking comes.
That in between the hearer and the heard,
hope may be brought, a purpose served,
You both will know, and knowing now, together find your
way.

*If you would like to hear the
reflection scan the QR code*

My own notes

Am I dying?

Am I dying. I can feel the weight of this question, even as I write. I can imagine the shock you may feel at the thought of what it would be like for you, if someone you love, or care for, asked you this. It may feel very daunting for you; seeing it written, or thinking about it being asked. So, firstly, maybe give yourself a chance to settle any feelings of panic, or fear, or heartache that has risen in you, from reading this. Maybe you need to leave this part for now, and come back to it when you feel more able, or ready. When you get a chance to steady yourself. It's alright to take your time here, this may feel very sore, so we will go as gently as we can.

In my experience, only a few people will ever actually ask this question. If they do, it is most often asked in the GP surgery, or by the side of a hospital bed, or during a clinic appointment with a consultant who has been treating the person. For those people living at home, or in a care home, who may not have regular contact with their doctor, they may ask you.

This question may not be asked directly, or as starkly as, "am I dying?" More likely, if it is asked at all, it will be asked more subtly, tentatively, in more searching ways. These more hesitant enquiries allow the person test out the water, test to gauge the hearing. So, in my experience, the question tends to come as some kind of almost throwaway remark, like, "I wonder is there any point in continuing with this treatment" or "I'm not sure I have much time left" or, "I think I'm nearly done", or, "do you think I'll get better".

These allow the person asking the question, feel their way into whether or not you are able for the question; able for the answer. And maybe even for the one who asks, a way to consider if they themselves are able for the answer. You may not be. For many of us, it is a question that is daunting in its enormity; frightening, overwhelming even. Conscious as we are, that the answer here, may very well be, a painful, honest "yes"

Where to begin; if you are asked this question, in whatever form it comes to you, a useful starting point may often be to check back with the person, wondering what has brought them to ask this question. What do they think is going on; how do they feel they're doing, how would they answer the question themselves.

Listening out for these cues is important and then picking up on them very gently, tentatively even, is a sensible way to proceed. Being tentative allows you to feel your way around the statement, what might the person mean. It also helps prevent you stumbling into an important conversation about dying and death, that the person didn't, in fact, intend.

The person might drop a cue to check out how you respond. Often, we want to fix, make things better, and it can be tempting to brush off any cue with an immediate reassurance or rush to minimise. The person then has a sense that any further attempts to have this important conversation with you, are not going to bear fruit. If instead, your response shows that you heard and understood, the person is able to note for themselves that you are able for such a conversation when they feel able to have it. And their timing is what is central here. The cue might simply be a way of testing out whether you are able for this conversation. And having tested this out with you, they may not continue any further at this point; and that's perfectly alright too.

Responses to the person's cues might be something like, "what's on your mind?" "Have you been wondering about the way things are going these past weeks?" Then wait.

So, having responded to the cue, and the person is ready to have this conversation, a useful starting point is, what the person already knows. "What have the doctors told you? What do you think is going on? What has brought this up for you at this time? Starting from what the person knows, helps ensure your responses aren't overwhelming, or that you are not breaking bad news that the person isn't actually aware of. If there are clearly gaps in what the person knows, you could offer to add in any information that you have. This is likely to be an emotional conversation, so do take your time with it. If this doesn't feel like something you could manage, or if you don't have any additional information, you could encourage the person to have a chat with their GP. The GP is well placed to talk through with them where they are medically.

Being alert for this question, however it is framed, and responding appropriately, is a valuable way of attending to more of what may be going on for the person . Allowing the person explore this question can help them begin to prepare for their dying and death. So, for example, there may be practical things they want to attend to; finances, funeral arrangements, making a will and so on. They may then feel able or ready to speak with those important to them; family, friends, carers. Furthermore, helping the person have this important conversation with you, can enable them consider those core spiritual or existential questions around their life's meaning and purpose, faith, hope, regret, love, fear and forgiveness.

Through your listening, your quiet witnessing, the person can give expression to what they may not have ever spoken of before. There may be opportunities for you to help allay some of the fears a person may hold. If they fear dying itself, for example, suggest they listen to the short BBC video recording where Dr Kathryn Mannix describes the dying process in a gentle, reassuring way, which might help. There may be opportunities to encourage the person speak with a chaplain, or a particular family member they are concerned about. You may be able to offer some suggestions on how to broach these conversations with people important to them.

Your role is valuable here. A deeply compassionate listening, without judgement, can be very therapeutic for the person; listening and trusting the person to share and say what feels appropriate for them. Stay alert too for when the person has had enough in the conversation, is tired or simply needs some quiet time for themselves to reflect. Allow them set the pace and the parameters and allow them finish up the conversation when they wish. Both they and you have a reference point now; a conversation that can be picked up again, if the person chooses. And if they don't, then that is there choice too.

I was asked this question. Three small words that held the world. And yes, it was very emotional, but it also held a gift for us. For in the asking and the answering, we were able to say to each other, some of those things that meant so much to us. We were able to say I love you; thank you; I'm sorry. I was able to reassure them that they would not be alone. This was especially important to the person. So, although this may sound and feel like a very difficult conversation, do trust that you will find your way in it. And maybe there's a gift that's waiting in for you too.

My own notes

32

Quick reference: Am I dying?

Start from what the person knows and work from there

Listen out for other more subtle ways that the question might be posed.

Respond according to the person's pace and timing.

Know that this will likely be a very emotional conversation.

There's no need to worry about being tearful and sad: there can be a great emotional release for you both.

This conversation could help the person, and you, prepare for their dying.

Reflection: Am I dying?

It doesn't often come so straight; so bare or blunt,
More likely couched in softer words or musings given voice.

"I think I'm tired of it all", can drift across a kitchen floor;
can reach and test and search its way, to gauge how it is heard.

Returned at once, with bold assurance, that there's long life still to live.
Or a pause that opens up the way for more.

There've been hours of silent wondering for the person who now asks,
And their speaking now will give them some release.

A tender conversation that will tug both your tender hearts
and touch in to what hopes or fears may linger in between.

May the courage that this moment asks, be available to you.
May it help you hold a space for further speaking.

May your listening turn to hearing, may your hearts hear what's not said,
And may you both find strength from here, to walk the days ahead.

If you would like to hear the reflection scan the QR code

My own notes

36

What should I say to the person who is dying?

These are very strange times for you, aren't they? Strange because this is so unfamiliar to you. Perhaps for the first time in your life, you are sitting this close to the dying and death of someone important to you. And I can imagine, you are carrying a lot, in your head and heart. Maybe you're thinking about things like caring arrangements, about medications, about visitors, about other family members, about your work. It's likely you also feel very tired, where for example, you have been travelling up and down to the hospital for visiting, or where you may be the main one providing care to the person at home. And perhaps your sleep isn't as restful or as constant, because you're worried, or you keep alert for any signs the person needs some help.

And this is a strange time too, because so many of the ordinary things you may have talked about before, feel too trivial now, unimportant, unnecessary. You may feel the significance of this time is such as to need space, and time, and words that somehow reach into, and out of your heart. That this time calls for a speaking and listening from your heart to theirs. A sense of solemnity as it were, that honours this important time. And that in itself can feel awkward or strange: talking about feelings, or saying I love you for example, may not be something you are used to.

We don't always need to use words. Very often we communicate through our actions, our behaviours. We are able to say, "I care", in how we are with this person.

The caring we provide, the fixing of the bed sheets, the plumping of the pillows, the offer of drinks or sips, the sitting quietly with, the holding of hands, the praying of prayers, the attentiveness to barely expressed needs, the many routine ministrations of love, or care, that we rarely think of. All of these speak of how we feel and how much we care. So, sometimes, words are not needed at all.

For some of you though, finding words is important, now that you recognise the person you are caring for, is nearing the end of their life. So, perhaps a useful starting point is for you to think about what it is that you want to say, or what it is that you feel you need to say, at this time. Only you can know what feels right for you.

Some people will reminisce in the presence of the person, recalling stories, adventures or events, that held some meaning to the person, or to the family. These can be quite spontaneous conversations, arising naturally. They may well create the doorway into speaking more tenderly about what the person means and meant to them. Others may talk about how the person was teacher, mentor, friend, cheerleader. There may well be tears and laughter here, and that is alright too.

Maybe you want to say something more. Maybe you feel you want to say I love you, or thank you, or I'm sorry, or I forgive you*. Some people say goodbye, or offer some kind of reassurance to the person that they can go. I know

* Developed from the traditional Hawaiian practice Ho'oponopono, of reconciliation and forgiveness.

that for many people, saying these things has brought them comfort in the days and weeks and months after the person has died.

Even if the person who is dying is in a very deep sleep, and maybe no longer rousable or responsive, they may well still be able to hear us, since hearing is one of the last senses we lose. Speaking to the person, therefore, can still be important.

Like so many of the questions that we are considering in this book, the answer here, very much depends on what works best for you. You might think through what feels alright for you in your particular family context, and in the relationships within your family. Some families are talkers, they talk about feelings, they showed their feelings and that was how they spoke in their family. Other families may be less inclined to speak about how they feel, or discuss family issues openly. So, when it comes to what to say when someone is dying, the usual or normal family patterns of relating in your family, will likely influence you.

This is an important time in the life of the person who is nearing death. And, it is a very important time for you. This is perhaps one of the last opportunities you may have, to speak with each other, or for the person to hear, at some level, what you say. So do take some time to think about whether, or what, you might like to say. There is no right or wrong, think about what feels alright for you. I know from my experience, that saying things like thank you, or I'm sorry, or I love you, or I forgive you, or goodbye, are very powerful things for us to say, and powerful things for us to hear. These are sentiments that are spoken from the heart, and it's in our hearts we hear them best. Speaking them, or hearing them, can soothe, and heal, and free us in so many ways. In this important time, trust that you will find the words you need and speak them from your heart.

Quick reference: What should I say to the person who is dying?

You may not wish to say anything in particular at all, and that's alright.

Think about what you would like to say, and if you feel able, say that.

If it helps, many people find it very comforting to hear or to say

I love you
Thank you
I'm sorry
I forgive you
Goodbye

Think about what works for you.

Reflection: What should I say to the person who is dying?

What word of mine can reach you now
That helps you on your way?
Or moves to you and in it's speaking
Helps me and we who stay?

What could be said that holds us both
In tenderness and care?
What message sent and understood
That both of us can bear?

If words do come then let them be
Some comfort in this time.
Some soothing balm, some healing grace,
for your soul and for mine.

May words of love and sorrow
Reach our hearing and our hearts.
I'm with you, and I thank you
Even as you now depart.

If no words come then may you know
the truth still manifest,
That light and love surround you now,
God grant eternal rest.

*If you would
like to hear the
reflection scan
the QR code*

My own notes

How might I spend the time with someone who is dying?

This may be the first time you are with someone very close to you who is dying. If this is so for you, then this can be very difficult, because of the sadness you feel, and because you may be already very tired from caregiving, and so many other responsibilities you may have. You may be wondering about what you should be doing, or saying, or attending to. Like so much of what we've talked about already, there is no right or wrong way to be with someone, at this time. For the most part here, you will do what comes naturally to you. You may well have an intuitive sense of how to be present with the person at this time. So, it is important that you trust your own inclinations to be quiet, or to talk. Maybe you can move more quietly around the person as you tidy up, for example, so that an air of calm surrounds the person. Some of these things tend to be what we seem to know and do already.

Perhaps it is helpful to consider here, some of the things that can affect, or influence us, in how we are here. It could be the closeness of our relationship with the person who is dying, for example, or how we express our feelings, or maybe even our relationships with others who are also present, and how they respond in this time. Where, for example, another family member is tearful and upset, you might feel you need to be more contained, or in control of how you feel; or careful in how you show your emotions. Or perhaps seeing someone else crying, may allow you feel more able to cry too.

Perhaps you may be sitting quietly, or maybe recalling stories of the person, or playing some music softly in their room. For some people, praying the prayers the person themselves prayed during their lives, is important to them at this time. Perhaps reading to them or telling them the tittle tattle of everyday news. So, if you feel able to be there, know that the person who is dying is likely to be very comforted by your presence.

There may be some practical things you can do to help keep the person who is dying as comfortable as possible. You may use pillows or cushions to support them. You may change their position if they are lying in the same position for awhile. This can help ease pressure on the skin of their shoulders, or back or bottom or heels. It's important too, not to move the person too often as this can be unsettling for them. If you aren't sure, ask your GP surgery or district nurse for advice and guidance.

For some of us, when we feel worried or upset, we can busy ourselves doing lots of different tasks, even if some of those aren't really that important. Keeping busy can help us feel useful, and may help us distract ourselves from the sadness or distress we feel. This is very understandable, and for many people, a normal way of coping with strong emotions. When the person we are caring for is so close to the end of their life, they will likely be very comforted knowing you are near, and that they are not alone. Although just sitting quietly with the person may not feel so busy, it is still a very caring and valuable thing to do.

I remember often seeing family members visiting with their loved one in hospice, during the years I worked there, massaging or rubbing the person's hands or feet. They sometimes used creams or pleasant smelling oils, where the staff had reassured these wouldn't cause any harm to the person. This can be a very gentle way of soothing the person and of showing your care. It can also help you feel close to the person. But it may not be something that you feel comfortable with doing, and that is alright too. Just being there, being present, can be enough.

If you are worried that the person seems to be in pain or distress, you can contact your GP surgery or district nurse and tell them. They will be able to offer some advice, or arrange to visit the person and ensure that some pain relief is given if needed.

It might feel alright for you, or another family member or close friend, to hold the person's hand. It can be very comforting to tell the person that you are there, that they are not alone, that you are with them.

I am conscious too, that for some of you, being with this person who is dying, is especially hard, because your relationship with the person hasn't always been an easy one: and may even have been very strained for years. For you, if you decide to be there, you may experience very mixed emotions, more complicated perhaps, than for those others who are with you at this time. It may be that you feel very torn; angry about what happened or didn't happen in the past; hurt that you didn't feel loved or cared for or protected; perhaps you are already grieving the relationship that you could have had, or should have had, with this person. This is very sore for you now.

So, for you, the expectations of those around you, can put extra pressure on you to be present in a certain way, to say or not say certain things. The invitation here for you, therefore, is to consider how best you can manage this already painful time. What do you feel able for? How can you hold the truth of what your experience of this person has been, alongside the fact that they are dying now.

Perhaps consider who or what can help support you best here. Consider how you can be true to yourself and your experience, and at the same time, honour, in as respectful a way as possible, the dignity of the person at this solemn time of their dying. These are huge considerations for you, so please do take the time you need, to prepare and resource yourself. We will look more closely at what to do if family relationships are very strained, later in the book. For now though, maybe think about what it might be like to be present, and find a way that works for you.

So, there is no right or wrong thing in how you spend time with the person who is dying. A quieter, slower pace of things does seem to help in this time. Words and activities that soothe and provide comfort to the person, like saying the prayers, holding their hand, or stroking their head, are likely very welcome. Little reassurances that you are there, even if the person isn't responsive, are valuable. Try not to worry too much, but trust that your intention, and generosity, in wanting to be a comforting presence to the person in this time, will guide you.

My own notes

Reflection: How might I spend the time with someone who is dying?

This is where surrender waits,
When certainty has run its course and
What we knew and know has paled.

It's like we're standing at the waters edge. Barefooted,
Where every swish and swash of even gentle waves
Will shift the sand and leave our standing sunken.

Resisting offers little here but fear
And so we step around to stand on firmer sand
Though wave on wave will bring more movement still.

If we can bow to this more fluid grounding,
And feel the breath within its ebb and flow,
Then maybe, in the swells, we'll hold a balance,
And find our feet firm standing once again.

If you would like to hear the reflection scan the QR code

My own notes

Do I have to be there at the end?

Put simply, the answer is, it's really up to you. There is no right nor wrong here.

People can have an image in their minds off what the scene around the dying person looks like. Often the image has been created by films that they've seen or books that they've read. So, for example, the image might be of a grieving family, some of whom have sped across the miles, travelled long journeys, to be there. The scene may show them sitting around the bed of the person who is dying; perhaps someone holding their hand, or some others crying softly. A general air of quiet calm and contained grief pervades. This image can suggest there is a 'right way' for this significant moment in any family, to be lived through. But families are different, people are different. Relationships between family members can be very different, and how your family manages this time, will be particular to you.

For some family members, or close friends of the person who is dying, this can be an important question. Maybe they feel unsure, or have mixed feelings, about whether they want to be present or not. Very often, the question hints at the struggle someone might have about the right thing to do, or what they believe is expected of them. So, for some people, thinking about being present can feel too scary or just too sore emotionally.

If you feel anxious or afraid about being present when someone important to you is dying, it might be helpful to ask a doctor what normally happens when someone is dying. Ask them what does dying normally look like. I talk more about this in another part of this book, so that might be helpful to read now, as it might ease some of your fear.

For some people, being present when someone they care about is dying, is important, while for other people, being present at that moment, isn't as important to them. There is no right or wrong thing to do here. The important thing is what feels alright for you? How might it be for you to be there? How would it be for you not to be there? And what do you feel able for. How might the choice you make here, be for you in the weeks and months afterwards? Whatever you decide, that is alright, and it is important to give yourself permission to choose whichever feels manageable for you.

I have known times when, even though someone wanted to be with the person who was dying, it didn't happen that way. I can remember times in hospice, when a family member may have stayed for hours, or days, in order to be with the person when they died. I remember occasions when they may have left the room for a comfort break, or to make a phonecall, or get a cup of tea, and the person died while they were out. Painful as this can be, we aren't always able to control whether or not we are present, and it may be helpful to hold this fact in mind.

It might be important to you, to take the time to say what you need or want to say to the person who is dying, if that feels alright for you. Perhaps to say your goodbye, difficult and strange as this may feel. It might be really helpful too, to let another family member know that you don't think or feel you want to be there when the person dies. This can relieve the stress and effort of people trying to contact you when the person is approaching their last hours of life.

Sometimes, things can move quicker than expected near the end of someone's life. This means it can be difficult to make sure, that you, or the people who want to be there, are there.

Try to remember it's not your fault if you can't make it. Death can be unpredictable, and it can be hard to know exactly when someone will die.

Do take some time for yourself now, to think through what you might feel able for, and whether you hope to be with the person when they die. Within the unpredictability of the time of dying, you will at least have some idea of what might work for you. Remember, there are different ways for us to be 'present' with the person who is dying. It may be that you are physically there with the person. It may also be, that for whatever reason you are not physically present, you may want to hold an intentional awareness of this important moment and time. You may want to hold a picture of the person, light a candle, play some music, say some prayers, as your way of 'being present to' the dying and death of this person who is important to you. You may want to be outdoors or go to spend this time at a place that mattered to the person while they lived, You may want to be with some others, some close friends, at this time, who can help you hold this sense of presence.

Give yourself some time to think this through for yourself, and choose then, according to what you feel you can manage or is helpful to you.

I had always hoped to be there, when my mother and my father died. As circumstances would have it though, I wasn't actually there with either of them. I was sad about this but am greatly comforted knowing that they each had some other family members there with them. So, even with the very best of intentions, and efforts, we aren't always able to be there. Sometimes, it feels like the person who is dying, has their own way, about whether anyone, or who, will be with them when they die. In the mystery of all that happens at this time, this too seems part.

Reflection: Do I have to be there at the end?

It's now, and now, and now again
In this place of quiet waiting. This time,
Marked out it seems, by each drawn breath.
An hour that follows hour that
Follows day that follows night.
This strangest time, for all who sit attentive, and who wait.
It's a way of being present too, that few of us
Have known before this time.
A 'being with' that lets us in to depth and breadth and width.
A 'presence to' in the presence of,
This one whose life is fading.
A texture rich, within the layers of all that happens here.
That 'presence to' may also hold
For those who choose or find themselves elsewhere.
A 'being with' that still allows them spend this time attuned.
Those strict confines of time and space
Are looser here. They're less defined and bridged instead
By thought, or heart, or hope.
May there be peace enough for all, within this 'presence to'.
May you find and feel how you'll be 'with', in close, or from afar.

If you would like to hear the reflection scan the QR code

My own notes

What if there is conflict / estranged relationships in the family?

When I was studying social work, in the late eighties, we had a text book called 'families and how to survive them'. I remember being struck at the time, that people's experience of growing up can be so different, and for some, very traumatic. Most of us recognise that relationships within and between family members can be both very supportive, and also very challenging. As very young children, and growing up, we test and learn ways of being in the world; what is acceptable here and what isn't, so for example, when I fall and graze my knee, is it alright to cry and seek comfort, or is that frowned upon and discouraged, by being told to toughen up or to stop whinging? We learn by how the behaviour is responded to. For the most part, we are really just trying to learn, how do I get my needs met in this family?

Parenting styles and attitudes can determine family culture; for example, how disputes between siblings are settled; whether or how feelings are expressed; how we see the grown ups in our lives manage their disagreements. What behaviours earn me rewards of love or encouragement, and what behaviours earn me chastisements, punishment, or a withholding of love?

I remember my younger brother telling me about a discussion he overheard between his three young toddler children and their newborn baby brother. These children were explaining to the baby, how things worked in the family! The oldest child, sage in his experience, explained how to eek out a later bedtime, by toddling or wobbling back up to his mum and dad, carrying his blanket, and quietly snuggling into the sofa beside his mum. The baby was being taught some of the basics of his family culture, some of the 'rules' of the house, by his three older siblings.

We know that some individual family members seem to be able to get on better together than with other members. We know that some personalities seem to clash more; that rivalries can grow between family members; that hurts and 'fall outs' can occur; we know that there can be perceptions of favouritism; that some traits or accomplishments are valued more highly than others. In some families, for example, being musical, or having a good sense of humour, can be regarded as more commendable or praiseworthy, than being interested in how tadpoles become frogs. There is layer upon layer of potential complexity within the dynamics of any given family. For many of us, we pay little attention to this, we give it very little thought, unless, that is, our experiences as children, have had a significant or detrimental impact on how we live our lives as adults.

For some people, tragically, 'surviving' growing up within or outside of a family, is very real. For some, living with the consequences of early childhood trauma, perhaps at the hands of an abusive family member, may require intensive, specialised, therapeutic support. If such as this has been part of your experience, I am so very sorry that this happened to you. And please, please, please, give careful consideration to whether or not, you attend at end of life of that family member. Take some time to think through how that might be for you; the impact that might have on you;

and what you might need, to support you, in and around this time. If there is a trusted person, or a therapist, you can talk to about this, it might help you discern what is best for you here; what feels safe and manageable for you. Thinking about yourself here, and what you need, is not selfish.

Some of you may be providing care to a family member for whom you feel little or no love. It might be from a sense of 'duty' or obligation, that you carry out a caring role. This is very hard for you, and can be even more difficult for you, and for other family members, when the person you are caring for approaches the end of their life. It can be especially jarring for you, when you hear others, health and social care professionals, for example, use the phrase, "your loved one", when they speak to you about the person you are caring for. Language really does matter to us, doesn't it?

Serious illness, and the dying and death of a family member, can feel like a crisis in any family system. It can be a very fraught time, even where family relationships are close and loving. When someone in the family is dying, there are the normal stresses that come from, for example, hearing the bad news; of making travel arrangements, of negotiating time off work, or other caring responsibilities. Perhaps there have been sleepless nights already, so people are tired, and with tiredness can come irritability or tetchiness. There may be any number of frustrations and difficulties, impacting individual family members and the family as a whole.

Where there are any small cracks in family relationships, perhaps created years ago, the crisis of serious illness or the end of life of a family member, can rupture these further. This can be a risky time for families. Perhaps family members who have been estranged, now as adults themselves, are brought back into contact, back into close proximity, and have to be around each other again. In this instance, those normal stresses and strains, that any family would experience at this time, can become amplified and weigh very heavily on all.

So, if you are in a situation where there is estrangement from other family members, or where relationships among you as a family, or with the person who is at end of life, are very strained, let's think about some of the things you might want to pay attention to; what might be the best you can hope for?, what might be helpful to you here?

One of the things, I think, that happens to us in a situation like this, is that we can become hyper aware. What I mean by this, is that we can be on high alert to see or hear any comments or 'looks' from the other, that we perceive as harsh and critical of us. We can be extra sensitive to any possible perceived slights, or judgements. It's almost like we are finely tuned to pick up further evidence from the other person, that confirms our belief that they continue to wound us, continue to judge us, continue to speak harshly and hurtfully to us or about us. Remember, you are likely very tired or under stress already in this situation, so your usual inbuilt barometer for measuring moods or tones, may not be as reliable as it normally is. In this stressful situation, it may be a little skewed towards hearing and seeing hurt, or interpreting what you see and hear as hurtful, harsh, or critical, because it is filtered through the lens of your past experience. It is, of course, also entirely possible that what you see and hear from that family member, is, in fact, hurtful or critical of you.

You may see or hear things that trigger memories of former experiences you had where you were hurt or harmed. These will likely come unbidden and will be hard for you to manage. Having a trusted friend to turn to for support, will be important for you. If you are able, give yourself some space and time to recover yourself. It could be a short walk outside, a sweetened cup of tea, a telephone call to a friend, for example. Whatever healthy options help you steady yourself again, give yourself permission to take that short time and space for yourself.

So, how would it be for you, to try and hold off reacting to what you see and hear as harsh or critical of you? How would it be for you, to give yourself some time before responding? I know this can be very hard, especially in the heat of the moment, and it may take a heroic effort on your part, so maybe think of it like this. By pausing before reacting or responding, you are able to hold your own ground, and perhaps choose, on your own terms, how you might or might not respond. Maybe it allows you ensure that your behaviour, or your reaction, is not dictated by the other person. Maybe this pause allows you stay true to yourself, and act more closely in accordance with your values.

This is a time where family members may be particularly vulnerable in themselves. Alongside the stresses and strains described above, they may also be trying to manage some very strong emotions . Some of the family members, you yourself, or indeed the person who is dying, could be experiencing deep regret about things that have happened. You could be grieving what could or what should have been. You could be suffering the heartache of missed opportunities for making better choices, or perhaps feeling shame or guilt at some of the choices that were made. These are powerful emotions to contend with, and could leave people feeling very raw. Any harsh word spoken into this, will cut very deep. Angry exchanges, or hurtful reactions here, could deepen the rift between family members, and make a future journey back towards repair, very difficult indeed.

It might also be perfectly sensible for you, in a situation such as this, that you step away from what you perceive as the bad behaviour of the other. It might be necessary for you to leave the room for a time, for example, so that you are not exposing yourself to the harshness, the hurt, the looks, that seem critical or judging, to you. It might be important for you to try and limit the amount of time you spend in the company of that other person. It might feel helpful for you to have someone with you who is a good support to you, someone who really cares for you. This can be especially important in a situation where you could feel overwhelmed, or powerless, in the face of bad behaviour directed towards you.

I remember working with a large family whose father was dying in hospice. There was a wide split within the family. The rupture had occurred many years prior to their father's admission to hospice. While their dad was still able to communicate his wishes, he was disinclined to be drawn in to the division, or to make any comment on it. There was so much hurt and pain within this family. It hadn't been attended to and had set like stone between the siblings. Their behaviours toward each other seemed to have set into patterns of hurting and being hurt. My work with this family concentrated on negotiating with them, a way to manage themselves in this time. A way in which they could have time with their dying father. A way to minimise the amount of time they were around each other. A way to behave, which was to agree not to shout or raise their voices in anger towards each other, in the presence of their dad, or in the hospice itself.

This may seem to you a very low bar, but, for this family, keeping to these agreements required a huge effort, and represented a major achievement. There was no magical reconciliation in this instance; no fairytale outcome of relationships repaired. There was, however, in the unfolding mystery of this time, the best that could be managed. For this family, in this time, the best that they could manage, was the absence of noise and disturbance around their father who was dying, which in itself, allowed for some semblance of peace.

You may be trying to manage a situation like this at home. Maybe for you, the person who is dying is being cared for in their own home, or in the home of another family member, or in a care home. Here, without the support of hospice staff, navigating such a fractured family relationship is likely much more difficult. So, lets think about what might be helpful for you in this circumstance.

Perhaps, as a starting point, it helps to try and keep your focus on the person who is dying, and what might be important for them, as they live out their final days. They are experiencing so many changes and challenges at this time. Physically, their bodies are slowing and gradually closing down. Socially, the energy and time they have for engaging with others, for visitors, is lessening. Emotionally, they are likely experiencing a world of feelings: sadness, fear, regret, hope, etc. and that too takes energy and space. Spiritually, they may be trying to make sense of what their lives have meant: what meaning they can make of the different twists and turns their lives had taken. Perhaps they're reconciling with the fact their lives are ending and all the losses and goodbyes that it entails. The person needs some time and space to manage all of these. Is it possible for you and for the other members of the family, to help ensure that the person has the time and space, and the peace they need, to manage this?

Another suggestion for you to consider is whether there is someone who could act as an honest broker in this situation. Perhaps an older relative or a family member in the wider family circle; an aunt, uncle, a second or third cousin. If this person is well enough regarded by you all, considered uninvolved in the disputes or disagreements that have caused the divisions in your family, they could help facilitate the flow of important information between you. Perhaps they could help propose and seek agreement for a schedule for visiting. Or maybe there's a priest or minister who could meet with you together, or individually, and help negotiate an agreeable way forward.

For you, maybe even wanting to try to include other family members feels too ambitious for you. So how would it be for you to begin at a further step back, to begin with wanting to want to try?

There is, of course, always the possibility that, at this solemn time of dying, a little space, some small opening up to healing, might come for you and for your family relationships. At this time, there could be moments offered where a path towards repair might open up. These could be small, generous acts of graciousness or hospitality on the part of even one person. I have seen these happen, where, for example, the person dying is being cared for by a family member in their own home. This carer, to all intents and purposes, could control access to the dying family member. This carer could control who visits, when they visit, how long they visit for. They could control the flow of, for example, medical information or updates, about the person's deteriorating condition. Where relationships are in conflict, issues of power and control can be present. When this main carer is able to recognise the importance of, and facilitate the visits of other family members to his or her home, this can be hugely restorative. Equally important here, and equally capable of creating a small shift in the fraught dynamic within the family, is that when those family members visit, they are mindful and respectful when they call.

When important medical information, about the family member who is dying, is shared with other family members in a timely way, this too can provide an opportunity for reciprocation in the simple gesture of acknowledging the communication. I have seen a softening of hearts for families, through these small acts of generosity, tentative and low key as they may seem.

So, what is possible for you? How can you manage yourself in this difficult place and time? Is there a moment offering itself to you, for a small, generous act of graciousness? Is there a possibility, remote as it may seem, for some little step towards a different way of being in relationship with your family? May it be so for you. May it be so for you all.

Quick reference: What if there is conflict / estranged relationships in the family?

This is a very stressful time for any family and strong emotions are likely present.

Think about how you might manage yourself at this time.

Think about whether or not you will be there.

If you decide to be there:

Think about having a trusted friend with you for support.

Take small, short breaks to have some time for yourself.

Try to hold off reacting: try to pause and choose how you respond.

Step away from bad behaviour.

Minimise the amount of time you need to be around the others.

Try to keep your focus on the person who is dying and what they might need at this time. (a calm environment)

Think about someone who could act as an honest broker for the family, to help facilitate agreements regarding appropriate behaviours or visiting schedules.

Think about how best important information can be shared with one another.

Try to notice any little moments or opportunities for even small positive gestures or generosity, towards one another.

Take care of yourself and do what you are able for.

Reflection: What if there is conflict / estranged relationships in the family?

And yes, it may be tight wrung hands that hold you in this place.
It's stark, and sharp and fragile thoughts that spill and fill this space.

You did your best with what you had, with what you knew back then,
To do your best in this time too, is what is asked again.

To find a way that honours you, is worthy of you now,
That you stay true yet do no harm is what will heal somehow.

No need for gestures, bold and big, that pain you to your core,
No empty words, no force no farce, no need for something more.

There may not be the textbook end, the hurt that's been undone.
Perhaps the grace that meets you here is strength to stand alone.

It wasn't as it should have been; it fell far short of right,
But standing at this crossing place, you choose to stand in light.

May you find solace on this ground, the smooth, and too, the rough,
You do your best, you do no harm, and that is good enough.

If you would like to hear the reflection scan the QR code

My own notes

Did the doctors tell me or did...? (When communication is hard)

Talking about anything that really matters to us, while important, can be difficult. Difficult because it's so close to our hearts. When the conversation is about someone close to us, especially if they are very ill or in declining health, then we are already likely to be feeling a world of strong emotions. Maybe we are fearful about what this illness may mean for them; maybe worried about how we see it affecting them; and most likely, we are uncertain about the future, for example. We can feel anxious to hear some news on how they are doing; eager to speak with someone for an update, or information on what is happening, or how they are doing. We will be keen to get some clear understanding of what is going to happen by way of a treatment plan.

Sometimes, on busy hospital wards, for example, it can be hard for us to find someone available to give us an update, to give us information. This can add to our concern. Having difficulty in getting information can happen too, if we are caring for someone at home. If we do manage to get speaking briefly with someone, we can feel that the information given to us seems vague or unclear, and we might be left feeling non the wiser.

About one year before my father died, he was rushed off to hospital late one night, with a life threatening aneurism which required immediate surgery. Although his situation was critical, he survived the surgery and was reported to be doing well.

Mam and I visited dad the next day and found him chatty and alert. We were asked to step outside while two physiotherapists set about helping dad sit out on the chair. From outside the curtain around dad's bed, mam mentioned to me her concerns that dad had a very poor colour. We became aware, still outside the curtain, of increasing staff activity around dad, and after some time, a doctor and nurse came to speak with mam and I.

A lot of things seemed to be happening very quickly. The nurse was quiet as the doctor talked and we listened but we were more tuned in to what now sounded like quite a number of staff in and around dad's bed, calling his name. In the midst of all of this, the message we picked up from what the doctor was saying, was that dad was being transferred to another nearby hospital, and we weren't unduly concerned. So, mam and I explained we would go home and other family members would be down for visiting time with dad that evening. The doctor did say a few times that we could accompany dad in the ambulance across to the other hospital. We remained content, however, that all was in hand and that we would go home. By this time, ambulance staff were helping the physiotherapists move dad onto the ambulance trolley. Activity and noise levels were high and by now, quite disconcerting.

The same nurse came back to mam and I and asked us if we understood what the doctor had said. I'm not sure how we answered, but thankfully she clearly recognised that we had not grasped the information given us, and offered to bring another doctor to explain things to us again. When she and the second doctor spoke with us, we understood that dad's condition had dipped significantly; that he was now critically ill, and that we should stay with him. The doctor suggested we call the rest of our family, to come to the hospital. We got such a shock, but we did as was advised. We were so grateful to that very perceptive nurse, who noticed that we hadn't grasped the seriousness of the situation, when the first doctor had spoken to us.

The rest of the family joined us and we stayed together with dad until his condition stabilised and he was out of danger. Dad survived this crisis and lived another good year. For so many reasons, Mam and I had not understood what the first doctor was telling us. We were two capable women; capable of listening, hearing and understanding information. In this instance, however, we were distracted by the flurry of activity around dad, concerned about what was going on, confused by the speed of change in dad's condition, and generally flustered by the comings and goings. The first doctor's communication style left it hard for us to pick up on some of the medical terms, or to decipher key information from what sounded like a lot of words. I was also conscious of the impact of this visit with dad, on my mam. Mam was herself, advanced in years, and had managed the long journey to the hospital, and the tiredness of walking long hospital corridors. These factors combined to leave us unable to understand what we were being told.

Mam and I very nearly left the hospital and dad, during what was such a critical time for him. Understanding the significance of what was being said to us, enabled us make the right choices for ourselves and for dad; to choose to stay with him when his condition was so serious that he could die.

Sometimes, we may be able to have a conversation with the person's GP or with one of the doctors treating them. While we will try to get some update on their health or condition, few of us may have considered that the update could bring disappointing or even bad news. Even if we harbour fears or suspect their health may be declining, we can still dread having our fears confirmed. We can still hold on to the hope that the doctor will allay our fears, reassure us that all is well, that all is in hand, for recovery back to reasonable good health. We can therefore, feel very unprepared, to hear a doctor explaining to us how serious the situation is for the person we are caring for.

This unexpected information can leave us feeling very shocked. Where this is the case for us, we might find it hard to concentrate on anything else that is being said. It might be really useful, therefore, to take some time to consider whether we are ready to hear the answers to the questions that we ask: to think about whether we want to know, when the news is not good.

Alongside all of this, for the medical professionals we may be coming in contact with, they are human too, and recognise the impact that bad news brings. They may feel hesitant or reluctant or maybe just anxious, to have to give the news that they know will cause you so much upset and pain. For the most part, their work has been focused on how to make things better for others, how to treat illness and improve health. They don't want to cause distress to family members or carers. In spite of this though, sometimes, they can't make things better; sometimes the news about the person's health or condition is very worrying. Sometimes the news is that the person won't recover, and it may be that the news they have to give is that the person may have a shorter time to live. So, for the doctors too, they may be coming to this meeting or conversation with you, with some anxiety. Anxious about how to tell you this sad news. Perhaps worried about how to find the right words to explain to you what is happening. They are likely to be very much aware of how upsetting the news is going to be for you.

We know from our own experience, that some people are really good at expressing themselves in clear, easy to understand ways. Other people are less so. We know that when some people feel rushed, or busy, or anxious, they can be less mindful of how they say something. We know too, how some professionals can speak using jargon or medical terms or technical language, that can be hard to make sense of. We know that some people use less direct ways of saying something, and that this can leave us unclear, or uncertain about what is being said or what is meant.

When we are enquiring about someone important to us, we do need help with understanding what exactly is being said, and what exactly it means. We need information that is easy for us to understand. We need time to take in what is being said and to ask questions about what is meant. We might need a slower pace in the conversation than we would normally, simply because this is so important. Our thoughts could be racing ahead, leaving it more difficult for us to stay focused on what else is being said. Just thinking about all of this then, we can begin to see how difficult this conversation might be. We can begin to see how hard it is for the one to give bad news, and how hard it is for the other person to hear it.

We have likely all known times, where we have been trying to explain something to someone, and, for whatever reason, they didn't fully understand what we were saying to them. We have also likely known times, in our own experience, where we have been listening to someone who is speaking to us, and have either not fully understood what they were trying to tell us, or have only heard some parts of what they were saying. We only have to think of some times when we were driving, got lost, and asked for directions. How clearly some people can describe the route to take, and how unclear the directions are from some other people.

Communication between people can, for so many different reasons, be challenging at the best of times. Where our hearts are so fully involved, as is the case when it's about someone we love or care for, communication can become even more complicated. This is because there are so many emotions, so many questions, so many racing thoughts, that it makes it very hard to listen and understand. In this, the worst of times for us and the person we care for, we need clear, paced, timely, and meaningful communication.

If this whole issue of communication is something you are wondering about, there are some things that you may be able to do to help in these important conversations. Perhaps write down for yourself, some of the questions you have, and any fears or worries you are holding about the person you are caring for. This can help you as a prompt during your conversation with the doctor. This can also help ensure you don't forget some of the questions you want to ask. Taking the time to think about the questions you have, might also help you prepare for this conversation.

Sometimes, this can help us think about and prepare for what the answers to our questions could be. "How will it be for me if I hear bad news?" When I take time to think about this, I can choose how much information I want the doctor to give me.

It might also be useful for you to think about whether you want to meet the doctor on your own, or with the person you care for. There may be some questions you would like to ask to help you in your caring for the person, or to help you make some plans; getting time off work, for example. Think about whether you want to bring another family member, or close friend with you. Some people have told me they worry that they won't remember all that is being said, so it helps them to have someone else with them.

Do persevere in getting to speak with someone, and if you need to try speaking with a different person, then that is alright too. Tell them what you are noticing in how the person you care for is doing. Ask them what this might mean. Tell them what you know already from conversations with other medical team members or health and social care staff. Ask them to explain to you what might be going on, and if you aren't sure what you are being told, ask them to say it in a different way, or to clarify what they mean. Maybe repeat back to them in your own words, what you think you've heard them say to you, then ask if you've got it right. Ask them if there are any other questions you should be asking, or any other important information you haven't thought to ask about. If you want to and feel able, ask them to speak frankly with you, in an open and honest way. Ask them to explain to you what happens regarding care, support and treatment from here on. Ask what information, if any, has been given to the person you are enquiring about. Maybe you could ask them for some guidance on how you might broach the subject with the person. As a summary of your conversation, you could ask them for the key pieces of information which are important for you to take away, or share with other family members or carers. Ask them about where you might get further updates or information if you need it.

This may all feel very cumbersome, or even awkward, in a conversation you might be planning on having. If it helps you to get the information you need, then perhaps it will prove worthwhile. My hope is that the doctors will carry the burden of this conversation by gently leading you through it. Your courage here will most likely be met by their courage to have an open, sensitive and honest conversation about someone really important to you. Together then, you will find your way into fuller understanding and preparedness for what may lie ahead.

Quick reference: Did the doctors tell me or did...? (When communication is hard)

Write down the questions you want to ask the doctor.

Tell them some of the things you're worried about.

Do you want to meet the doctor on your own or with the person you are enquiring about?

Do you want to bring someone else along with you, to help you remember what was said?

Tell them what you are noticing in how the person you care for is doing. Ask them what this might mean.

Ask them to explain to you what might be going on, and if you aren't sure what you are being told, ask them to say it in a different way, or to clarify what they mean.

Ask them if there are any other questions you should be asking, or any other important information you haven't thought to ask about.

Ask them to explain to you what happens now, regarding care, support and treatment from here on.

Ask them what are the key pieces of information which are important for you to take away, or share with other family members or carers.

Ask them about where you might get further updates or information if you need it.

Reflection: Did the doctors tell me or did...? (When communication is hard)

Words will move like water, soft or loud.
A drip, drip, drip, become a rush and gush
to say what needs be said.

May meaning meant, be meaning made, within this flow.
May understanding settle, cool and clear.

May thirst to know be quenched by this new knowing.
May words, like water, soften, soothe and ease.

If you would like to hear the reflection scan the QR code

My own notes

Why are they talking about resuscitation? (DNACPR conversations)

This question may never come to you. For those of you, caring for someone close to you at home, the question may never arise. But for others of you, especially where the person you are caring for has been admitted to hospital, the doctors might need to broach this subject with you and with the person themselves. It is an important question and a very delicate one. It introduces a subject that has been poorly understood or, in some cases, may have been poorly explained and talked through.

Across the course of my work, I have listened to people describe with great distress, the why and how of this conversation about resuscitation. They sometimes described their shock when the Doctor who was responsible for the care of the person while in the hospital, raised this question with them. Some people described how they felt hearing this subject raised, made them think the doctors were 'giving up' on the person, or 'stopping treatment'. That the conversation meant they were going to do no more, and just let the person die.

Some people described their fears that it was only discussed with them because the person they cared for was very advanced in years; because they were considered old and therefore not worthy of lifesaving treatment. Thinking that this is what is happening will cause so much pain and hurt. It may also cause mistrust or conflict between the family and the doctors treating their loved one. For these reasons, understanding more about resuscitation, can dispel some myths, and help ensure the conversation with the doctor is clear and understood.

So, first of all, having this discussion does not mean that treatment of the person you are caring for will stop. It does not mean that the doctors are 'giving up' on the person. It does not mean that the person will simply be left to die without appropriate care, support and treatment. The discussion will only be introduced to the person, based on that person's overall condition, and concern for that person. It is not applied to whole groups of people based on , for example, their age, or their ability. This discussion, if introduced to you at all, is specific to the person you are caring for.

The Resuscitation Council UK provides valuable information on this subject, in a clear and easy to understand way. They have a website which you may like to visit, and read for yourself the detail provided there. They explain the when and how of resuscitation. They offer the facts on when and how often resuscitation is successful in restarting the heart. The website answers many questions, that you will likely find very helpful, in relation to resuscitation, if it has come up for you, and the person you are caring for.

For many of us, our ideas about resuscitation are formed from watching hospital dramas on television. While the drama, the frantic activity, the heroics, the outcomes, make for compelling viewing, unfortunately they don't often reflect real life. In fact, they can seriously skew our notion of what CPR is and when it might be appropriate.

Most of us do know that CPR seeks to restart the heart when the heart has stopped pumping blood around the body. The person will have stopped breathing and will have become unresponsive. It is a very forceful and intrusive intervention. The heavy pressure applied to the person's chest, can for example, cause fractures to the person's ribs. Or where electric shocks are used, it can cause the person's entire body to jolt. CPR is likely to be very distressing to watch, if it is being done on someone close to you.

The doctors who are treating the person, are making their assessments based on a lot of medical information. They are trying to create a clear overall picture of how the person is doing medically. Based on this overall picture of the person's condition, they are trying to weigh up the most appropriate treatment for the person at the time. Sometimes different types of treatment have benefits and harms. The doctors try to make their decisions about treatment, based on where any potential benefit outweighs any potential harm.

If the doctor is introducing the subject of resuscitation to you, or the person you are caring for, it will be based on their medical assessment of the person at that time. This assessment will include any clear indications that the person's health or condition has gotten worse, or where it is expected to get worse. It will include whether attempting CPR is likely or unlikely to be successful. It will also include whether any potential harms of attempting CPR outweigh any potential benefit. The doctors will consider if it appropriate when the overall medical assessment of the person's condition, is indicating the person is already at, or close to, the end of their life. In this instance, the doctors would recognise that beginning CPR, when the person's heart does stop, would be to interrupt, in a very intrusive and likely futile way, the normal dying process.

The doctors will want to discuss this with the person to help the person understand their overall medical condition, and for the doctors to understand the person's wishes, feelings, beliefs and values, in relation to this information. They may well invite you to join in that discussion. Sometimes, if for some reason, the person isn't able or doesn't want to have that discussion with the doctors, you may be asked to help them understand what the person would have wanted, or if the person had ever spoken to you before now, about their wishes.

This discussion will be hard for you, and you could feel very upset. If you want, you can of course, ask any questions you might have. You might be able to tell the doctors about any conversations you have had with the person, about what care, support and treatment they would want, if they were very ill, so ill that they could die.

If this discussion has been introduced to you, and you feel a churn of so many feelings and worries, that is very normal. This is an important discussion with the doctors, and, if you feel able, it can really help to ensure that the person you are caring for, is not burdened with an intrusive, undignified and likely futile medical intervention, as they come to the end of their lives. It will reassure you also to know, that all appropriate care, support and treatment will continue to be provided to the person you care for. Such reassurance will be a great source of comfort to you and to the person you care for. So, while this conversation will be sore, it will also be a very valuable one and help you in your caring for the person.

Image used by kind permission of Anita Hoy

Reflection: Why are they talking about resuscitation? (DNACPR conversations)

Look up.
Even when the colours can't be seen,
That same big sky shelters all you love.

*If you would like to hear the
reflection scan the QR code*

My own notes

Why can't they eat or drink?

Although we may not often think on it, eating and drinking forms a central role in our lives. Perhaps when we're young, it may feel more functional, necessary fuel for our bodies, to build energy and strength, to lead our lives. For special occasions though, like birthdays or anniversaries, or important family celebrations, preparing and sharing favourite foods allows us come together to mark the occasion. Its not surprising then, that we often associate providing food, or cooking tasty meals, with showing love, or caregiving.

In our later years, eating and drinking can take on new significance, marking as it does the hours across the day: the breakfast time, the lunch time, the dinner or tea time. These signifiers of the passing of time can hold a meaning beyond any functional aspect. Where other physical or social activities become less manageable, there's still the meals to share and eat.

When someone is coming closer to the end of their lives, they can become much less interested in eating or drinking, and often times their appetite may lessen. They may eat smaller portions, or maybe even skip some meals altogether. For you, this can be difficult, and you likely want to encourage them to eat by making those favourite foods they used to enjoy. Perhaps you worry too that they must keep eating to keep their strength up, and be better able to ward off illness or weakness, or to recover from a recent decline in their health. Seeing them eat so little can be hard for you, so it may be helpful to understand what may be going on. The main thing for you is that you do continue to offer the person small, tasty, bites of food or sips of drinks. To offer when appropriate but not insist or force.

As someone is nearing the end of life, in the last weeks or days or hours, it is normal that they don't eat as much or maybe don't eat at all. This is because their body is already slowing down and they don't need as much energy. They are likely sleeping a lot more, likely not to feel hungry and much less likely to try to eat or swallow food. As their body continues to slow down, their ability to digest food also slows down and it might even feel uncomfortable for them to have food in their stomach.

It is always important though, that if you are worried there may be another reason why the person isn't eating or drinking, you speak with their GP to talk through your concerns. Perhaps for some of you, if the person you are caring for has been seen and assessed, the doctors, or a speech and language therapist, may recommend some modifications on food and drink. This could be because they notice the person's ability to swallow is becoming very weak. Maybe they noticed the person trying to take their tablets or take a drink, and that it causes them to cough a lot, or causes them discomfort.

If we don't understand why some modifications have been recommended, about what the person you care for eats or drinks, then it can seem really harsh to you. I remember some people telling me they were worried or angry about these recommended modifications. They feared the person was being starved. So, it is always important to have good clear information on what is being recommended or suggested, to help you understand and reassure you.

The way it's been explained to me, and how I've come to understand it, is this. We have all likely experienced at some time or another, that when we're eating or drinking, we get a coughing fit. It can even make our eyes water. We usually say, "it went down the wrong way". What has likely happened to us here, is that some small particle of what we were eating or drinking, actually went down our 'windpipe'. Our 'windpipe' as we call it, leads directly into our lungs, and our lungs definitely aren't meant to deal with food or drink. Our lungs are focused on our breathing. So, if something went down the wrong way, we cough hard to try to clear it. It isn't a pleasant experience for us, but because our cough is strong, and we are bright and alert, it doesn't last too long and it doesn't happen to us very often.

The person you are caring for though, may not be as bright or alert if they are coming to the end of their lives. Their swallow may be weakening, either because of their particular illness, or just as their overall condition weakens. The risk of something they are eating or drinking 'going down the wrong way', could be more likely, or it could happen more often. Again, because they may be weaker overall, their ability to cough may not be as strong or as effective. The bout of coughing itself could be exhausting for them, and could leave them feeling sore from the effort. There is also a risk, then, that whatever particle did 'go down the wrong way', if their coughing doesn't clear it, they could get a chest infection for example, as a result. As we know, a chest infection, or recurring chest infections, can also be very hard on the person, their breathing is affected.

In this light then, we may be able to see why some modifications on eating and drinking might be recommended. They are intended to help prevent the person from experiencing food or drink going down the wrong way, which causes or can cause discomfort. Any modifications that have been recommended by health care staff, are not suggested so as to starve the person, or stop them from enjoying certain foods, but to try to ensure that the person remains as comfortable and as well as is possible.

If the person you are caring for is very near to the end of their life, then how much or how little they eat and drink will not really change how much longer they live. There are still things you can do that will help though. You may like to help keep the person's mouth and lips moist, so if they are able to manage, small chips of ice or frozen juice can be very refreshing. If they want to, and are able to, help them to take regular sips of drinks, or maybe use a little moistened mouth swab if their mouth feels dry. Speaking with your local health centre or district nurse for advice, will guide you here, as to what is appropriate at this time, for the person you are caring for. You can feel content then, in knowing that what you are doing, is helping keep the person as comfortable as possible.

My own notes

Reflection: Why can't they eat or drink?

And maybe what we hunger for isn't different here.
And what has nourished all along sustains us still.
Our needs the same as we live out these days.

That we feel sheltered, safe and free from any harm.
That gentle hands provide our care, and tend us while we sleep.
While washed and dressed our pace is kept, our dignity maintained.

That when we fear, we're heard and soothed;
our grief allowed to show itself and weep.
That, if in pain, relief will come, our suffering be bourne.

That we hear tones of tenderness where our name is spoken;
That kindness lights the eyes that look our way.
That peace may find it's way to us and stay.

That we belong and feel at home, at ease in who we are.
content with how we lived the life we had;
That the legacy we leave is as we hoped.

That we are grateful, all in all, for what we chose,
That mercy holds all else we might still rue.
That we're embraced by love as we take leave.

So, surely what we hunger for isn't different here,
And what has nourished all along sustains us still.
Our needs the same as we live out these days.

If you would like to hear the reflection scan the QR code

How will I know: What can I expect?

This may be the first time that you have been close to someone who is dying. You may feel unsure about what to expect, or maybe feel worried or fearful. Having some understanding of what will likely happen, what you might notice, can be helpful, and may ease some of your concerns.

People are different, and there can be some differences in how people die. There are also, though, some common signs that show the person is coming to the end of their life. These changes may be happening gradually over months or weeks, and sometimes, they can be hard to notice because they are so gradual. For some people, these changes can seem to happen quite quickly, in a very short period of time. Even where the person has become very unwell more suddenly, and a marked decline is evident, we may still see some of the signs described below, as they tend to be a natural part of the dying process.

When I think of my own experience of those closest to me who died, I can now recognise that they went through some of these very natural changes over the course of their last year of life. I also reflect on the fact that how they actually died was different. My dad died very suddenly in the end, although his health had been in decline for the previous year or two. On the morning he died, he was bright and alert, and talking with my mam and sister. Quite suddenly, he became very unwell and died within an hour or two. My mam's decline was much more sudden, but it was rapid, and she died over a few days. So, while you can't be certain about how the person you care for will die, we can look at some of the more common signs, that may indicate the person is moving closer to their dying.

Eating and drinking less

You may have noticed already that the person you are caring for doesn't seem as hungry, or as interested in eating or drinking very much. This can be hard for you, because often we show our love or care for someone, by providing tasty food, preparing the things they like to eat, to try to encourage them to eat or drink more, and, as we see it, keep up their strength. People who are coming to the end of their lives don't need as much energy from food, and do not need to eat and drink as much as when they were healthy and well. Seeing someone you love, eat or drink so little, or maybe even stop eating, can be very hard for you to accept, but this can be a natural part of the body slowing down.

If you notice this, it's important to take into account any advice or guidance you may have had from health professionals, who are involved in the person's care. You may want to speak with your GP and describe what you are seeing here. The GP may be able to assess the person and ensure that there isn't any medical reason for their loss of appetite, which could be treated. This check can help you understand that the person is less interested in eating and drinking because they are moving towards the end of their lives, rather than for any medical reason.

So, maybe you could let the person you are caring for, eat and drink as much or as little as they want. Sometimes, this may be as little as a few sips or a few small spoonfuls. It is good to still offer the person something to eat or something to drink, encouraging them but allowing them turn your offer down. When someone is at this stage of their lives, it is alright if they don't want anything at all. Sometimes people stop eating days or even a couple of weeks before they die.

Sleeping More

You may also have noticed that the person seems to spend a lot more time sleeping. Sometimes, this sleep can be so deep that the person is hard to rouse if you try to wake them. Again, this is a normal part of coming towards the end of our lives, as our bodies are slowing down. At the very end of our lives, this sleep can be so deep that we are not rousable at all. We can spend a few days or even longer like this, before we die.

During this time, we believe the person is likely still able to hear, since hearing is one of the last senses we lose before we die. So, it can be comforting, to continue speaking with the person, letting them know you are there, telling them who else is around, and reassuring them.

Talking less or becoming quieter in themselves

Another thing you may notice in the person you are caring for, is that they become quieter in themselves. Maybe they don't talk as much or engage in conversations that are happening around them. Maybe they're less inclined to read the newspaper or watch television or listen to the radio. You may be spending a lot of time with the person, and notice how quiet they are in your company. Then, when another family member or close friend arrives to visit, you can be surprised at how much the person does talk, and seem so interested in what's going on. While you may well feel very pleased to see these interactions, you could also feel disappointed, because the person stays so quiet when others aren't around. In my work, I have some times heard carers say how hard it is for them, that the person seems to save their best for others who call, but for them there's little conversation or interaction.

If we think of it like this though; talking and listening takes a lot of energy. Even when we are healthy, listening and talking can be exhausting. So, maybe the person you are caring for feels so content in your company, that they know they can be quiet with you. They know they don't have to try to be sociable, they know they can say as much or as little as they feel able for.

For some of us though, such quiet can feel very strange. Perhaps we're not used to longer periods of silence between people. Perhaps we feel a bit awkward or uneasy in the quiet, especially when we're with someone else. Maybe we feel we should be filling this space with talk or chat. How would it be for you, to check with the person what works for them? Perhaps you could agree to play some music quietly in the background, or have the television or radio on, but at a lower volume? You're trying to find a way that feels comfortable and manageable for both of you. A balance of quiet and conversation, of silences and sounds. Companionship can sit contentedly within either of these. Find the way that works best for you.

As the person moves closer to their last days and hours.

In their last days or hours of life, the person may tell you that they saw or heard someone, who you know has already died. They might mention that their own deceased mother or father or close relative had visited them. They might mention that they could see them or hear them. Or you may notice the person looking, as though at something that you can't see. These may not be any kind of hallucinations related to medications, but may, as many believe, be part of the process of taking leave of this world. It may be something like, they are having a sense of the closeness of others whom they loved in life, who have already gone before them. This experience can be very comforting for the person. Again, if you are concerned about this, or think the person is distressed by any of this, you can speak with your GP for advice and reassurance.

Changes in breathing

As the person comes to the last days and hours at the end of their lives, there may be some new signs that you will notice. One of these is that the person's breathing will change. It may slow down and have long spaces between breaths, or it may sound very laboured. Their breathing can become noisy and make a rattling sound. You may think this is distressing and uncomfortable for the person, that they need to clear their throat. While this may be hard for you to witness, for the person though, they are now in such a deep state of unconsciousness that it doesn't bother them. These changes in breathing might only start a few hours before someone dies, or they might last for a few days; everyone is different.

Restlessness and agitation

Sometimes a person can become restless or agitated. You may, for example, notice them pulling at the bed clothes. This does not necessarily mean the person is in pain or distress; it may simply be an outward sign of some of the changes that are happening inside the persons body; the slowing down, and closing down, that happens before we die. If you are worried though, that the person may be feeling pain, do contact your local health centre and explain what is happening. The GP may be able to give you some reassurance or prescribe some medication to be given to the person, to help manage these symptoms well.

Cold hands and feet

At this stage too, the very end of life, you may notice the person's hands or feet become cool to touch, and their colour can become much paler, or look a little blue. Again, this can be very normal, as the person's circulation is slowing down and there is less oxygen reaching their hands and feet. You could add a blanket or put thick socks on the person to help keep their feet and hands warm. At this stage, the person themselves is unlikely to feel this cold, but I know it might be something you would like to do.

As I mentioned already, people are all very different, and it is very difficult to know, or to say exactly, how or when someone will die. Some of the signs I have described, taken together, do often suggest that someone is moving closer to their dying. These can be fairly typical indicators that are often seen, in what some describe, as normal dying; when a person has come to the end of their life. If you feel unsure, or if you have concerns, a conversation with the person's GP will very likely help. Clear information, having your questions answered, having your concerns listened to, can be reassuring even if the answers are hard to hear.

Knowing what is happening with the person you are caring for, can help you make choices about what is important now. Knowing, can help you focus on for example, how you spend your time with the person, or how much time you spend with the person. It can help you think about whether there are other family members you might need to speak to. Having a better understanding here, can help you prepare for the time ahead, help you prepare yourself. And so, while it takes great courage for you to ask this question, good information can be very valuable to you. So, do ask your GP, or maybe you could speak to a knowledgeable and experienced nurse. Knowing, when you are ready to know, that the person you are caring for is close to dying, can be a great support to you at this time.

My own notes

112

Quick reference: How will I know, What can I expect?

When someone is approaching end of life, you may notice some physical and emotional changes in the person.

Changes in eating and drinking

Sleeping more

Maybe becoming quieter, more withdrawn

In the last days and hours, you may notice some more changes:

Unable to be roused from sleep or unresponsive

Changes in breathing or noisy breathing

Restlessness and agitation

Cold hands and feet

Reflection: How will I know, What can I expect?

We reach the edge of knowing, here
This crossing place from life to death.
A threshold space, where mystery weaves and
Works, unknown, unseen by we who stay.

We reach the edge of knowing, here.
This taking leave and letting go.
What final tasks completed here,
What closures brought, what endings done.

We reach the edge of knowing, here.
What faith we have surrounds and holds,
While we keep watch. This waiting time
Is filled and full of all our hearts can bear.

We reach the edge of knowing, here.
And so, we pray, we hope, we wish, we want,
That all be well for this one now
Who takes their leave, then turning still, goes on.

May we who've reached this edge of knowing
Feel the Grace that awaits us here.
May there be comfort in the presence of this mystery.
May easement come.

*If you would like to hear the
reflection scan the QR code*

My own notes

What about when my time comes, how can I try to get what I would like?

Like many of you, I have often over the years gone to a wake, or a funeral, to pay my respects to the person who has died, and to offer my condolences to their grieving family. It is fairly common at these times, to hear, among so many other things, the family or friends of the one who has died, tell and retell the story of the person's last illness or to talk about the circumstances of their dying.

It isn't that surprising really, that when we attend a wake or a funeral of a family friend, a relative or a neighbour, we may begin to think about our own mortality. Or, perhaps we find ourselves thinking, as we listen to the stories told during the wake and funeral, about the circumstances of that person's dying and death. Some of the stories told may have described a peaceful dying, or that the care given to the person was really good, for example, and some stories may have described more difficult experiences. Reflecting on these could make us think about how it would be for us if we found ourselves in similar circumstances, when we reach our end of life.

Perhaps, like me, you have sometimes heard people comment quietly to another, something like, "well I wouldn't want that", or "he never would have wanted that", or "I'd like something like that when my time comes", or "if I had my way I'd make sure that….". These are sometimes things like particular hymns chosen for the funeral, or whether there is a picture of the person standing on or near the person's coffin. Sometimes they might be about more significant issues such as certain types of treatment the person would or wouldn't want, or whether they would want to be cared for in their own homes, or in a care home, at the end of their lives.

These are important things for us to think about. There are some things we can do that could help us try to ensure that what we would like or want is, in fact what happens when our time comes. A starting point would be to think about what we would want and hope for, when that time comes. This isn't about trying to foretell our future, none of us know what lies ahead for us. Instead, it is about us taking some time to think about what is really important to us now, as we live our lives, and then to try to think ahead to what might be really important for us when we come to the end of our lives.

Thinking ahead or planning ahead isn't that unusual for us. When you think of some of the decisions you've made over your lifetime; opening a bank account, or taking out a mortgage, thinking about getting married, or thinking about starting a family of your own, or buying a house, maybe planning a change of jobs, or taking out house insurance, all of these require that we do some planning ahead, and make some provision for our future. So, it might be helpful to think about this, as planning ahead to make some provision for our future care, support, and treatment, when we reach the end of our lives.

A number of years ago, I called in to see my mother and father on my way home from a funeral I had attended. It was a bitterly cold winters day and mam and dad were sitting in their usual chairs, at either side of the fire. They would have gone to the funeral themselves had they not been recovering from heavy colds. With fresh cups of tea in hand, I described what was a beautiful funeral liturgy, and also some of the people I was speaking to there.

As I recounted some details of the liturgy, Dad mentioned at one stage, that he would like something similar when his time came. He was quite specific in a couple of regards, so I asked if he would like me to make a few notes on this. I explained that I could tell my sister and brothers that I had these notes of what he and what mam said. Then, when their time came, we all knew what they had said they wanted. Mam and dad thought this was a good idea, and they proceeded to add more and more things to my list. There were a few differences in what they mentioned, so I noted those too.

Some of the conversation had us laughing out loud, and some of it was quite emotional and had us tearful. We managed our way through these layers of feelings, as families often do, not taking ourselves too seriously, and holding the solemnity of what we were discussing, as lightly as we could. When they seemed to have finished, I read my notes back to them. With a few minor changes here and there, we boiled the kettle once again, and talked of other things.

I told my sister and brothers about the conversation and that I had the notes. I didn't need to give any detail about the content at that time. It was enough to let them know that mam and dad had told me what they wanted when their time came to die. During a visit a few weeks later, dad mentioned a change he wanted to make in relation to one thing he had said, so I noted that accordingly. I was struck by the fact that he had obviously given it some more thought since the day we had first discussed it.

When dad came to what was the last year of his life, I offered him opportunities to revisit that conversation we had had all those years ago. On each of these occasions, dad declined. This wasn't something I needed to force at all, it was enough to offer and allow dad decide if he wanted to say more or not. When he died, and after we as a family had met with the undertaker, I was able to share with the others, what dad had stated as his wishes. For each of us, knowing what dad had wanted, and carrying out his wishes, gave us great consolation. For a big family, such as ours, there could have been many differences of opinion about what we should do or how we could mark dad's dying and death. The potential for disagreement can be huge at a time like this, especially where grief is present. For us though, there was no dispute or vagueness about what his wishes might be. It was clear from that conversation all those years ago. We were in no dilemma and were guided entirely by what dad's stated wishes were. The knowledge from that conversation was a real gift to us in the midst of our mourning. Being able to honour his wishes was a great comfort to us all.

Sometimes, of course, as was the case for mam, circumstances were such, that one of mam's stated wishes, couldn't be carried out. While very disappointing, we recognised, as did mam, that in this particular regard, we needed to do the next best thing. And this we did.

I'm telling you this personal story to help explain what we're talking about here. From my experience, you can see how useful it can be to talk with someone close to you about what your wishes are, so that people are clear, in that time in the future, when you may not be able to make your wishes known. For those closest to you, knowing what you consider is important to you, when you come to the end of your life, is very valuable information. We don't know for sure what will happen for any of us, but we can begin to think about some of the things we would want or not want to happen. This is especially important, if, for example, for whatever reason, at some time in the future, we weren't able to make our wishes known.

If you think this is something you would like to explore further, you can ask your GP about it. Health and social care professionals call this type of planning ahead, Advance Care Planning, and they will be able to guide you. You may like to visit your local government health department website to check what information and guidance they have to offer on this. Where I come from, we have a dedicated section on our department of health's website called Advance Care Planning: For Now and For the Future, which is helpful and easy to understand. I will add some website links for you, at the end of the book.

In the meantime, it might be enough for you to think about what you could do now. Sometimes, it might feel more manageable to begin with something that feels more comfortable for you. Some people, for example, find it easy enough to think about a favourite piece of jewellery, or a much loved book, a family heirloom, a album of special family photographs, and then think about who they would like to have it, after they are gone. Something like making your will, or maybe some tentative ideas about what type of ceremony or hymns or readings you would want for your funeral. Sometimes, these more manageable tasks, can be a doorway, through which we can step, into more detailed considerations. Perhaps you could begin to think about the kind of care or support or treatment you would want, or not want, if you were very ill, or approaching your last weeks or days of life. You might think about for example, some of the different types of medical interventions that you would or wouldn't want to have. You might be able to think about organ donation. You might want to think about where you would prefer to be cared for, or who you would like to be involved in your care, at that time.

Thinking about these things now, when you are well, and telling someone close to you, can ease your mind and unburden you of some of the worries you might carry about your future. It can also help those closest to you, to have confidence and comfort, in knowing what you would want. They might feel more able to tell doctors, or other people who may be involved in your care or treating you, what you would want, if something happened to you, or you became so ill that you weren't able to make your wishes known.

For me, one of the most valuable things about this kind of planning ahead, is that it allows me take some time now, to think about what's really important to me. It allows me some time to think beyond the normal, everyday, stresses and strains of life and living; of paying bills, buying the groceries, arranging child care, for example. In my work, when I have helped people think and talk through advance care planning, they sometimes mention that what is really important to them are things like spending time with family. Others may reflect on the importance of spending time outdoors, being close to nature. Sometimes people talk about their beliefs, their faith, their values. If we do take some time to think about these things now, then we can begin to ensure that the choices or decisions we make about, for example, how we spend our free time, align with our values and our beliefs, and we are able to live our lives in accordance with these.

It is also possible, that you might change your mind, of course, about some of these things, so you could revisit this conversation with those closest to you, and make any changes.

For doctors, or other staff involved in treating you, where, for example, you became critically ill, knowing what you have said you would want, or not want, is valuable information. This helps them take into account your wishes, when making any clinical decisions. It also helps them have a real sense of you and what matters to you. They gain a little insight from this information into the type of person you are, your values, your beliefs, your feelings, your wishes. For those closest to you, it provides them with so much more confidence in being able to tell the doctors what you had talked about, and what you would or wouldn't want. This can be very reassuring and comforting for them, especially if the doctors are asking them questions about your views on some particular types of medical interventions or treatment.

Reading some of this may seem odd to you. Odd, because so many of us trust that our doctors will make medical decisions that are best for us. We also know that sometimes, deciding on which course of treatment to undertake, isn't always clear cut. A very simple illustration might help us here. The doctors could be thinking something like, if we start treatment X, it might have a negative effect on the patients condition Y. And maybe that negative effect could seriously impact on, for example, the patients ability to be independent. So, the doctors are trying to weigh up the benefits and burdens of different treatment options which may or may not be best at a particular time. To follow this simple illustration further, let's say you have thought through what you would or wouldn't want, and have spoken to those closest to you about that. Let's say, for example, you said that being able to stay as independent as possible, for as long as possible, is really important to you. If the doctors know this, then they can see that risking treatment X, may not be in keeping with your wishes. Any guidance therefore, from what you have said, is really helpful to them, and they can include it, alongside all the other medical information they have available, in making their clinical decisions about what is best for you, at this time.

Many people tend to agree that this kind of planning is a good idea, but for so many reasons, only a few actually do it! Maybe they just never get around to it, or maybe they think they'll do it when they're older, or when they're ill, or any other time but now. For my dad, it was a conversation he was happy to have when he was in very good health. Years later, when his health was deteriorating, he didn't want to re-visit the conversation. Perhaps by that stage, he felt it might be too hard to think and speak about.

May I encourage you here, to take the time now, to think about what is important to you in your life, and try to think about what might be important for you in the future, regarding your care and treatment. Think about your wishes, feelings, beliefs and values, and what you might or mightn't want, if you became ill, and were unable to communicate these yourself. Think about those close to you, and who you could talk to about this. Begin with something that feels manageable for you.

However you choose to begin, however tentative that first step, however self conscious that first conversation might feel, the important thing is, to begin.

Reflection: What about when my time comes, how can I try to get what I would like?

Is there a time within this time, that is the right time?

A time of day or time of night?

Or, in the year, a time that might create a planning time?

What time within your life of time, or time of life,

Will you make time to think upon 'that time'?

If you would like to hear the reflection scan the QR code

My own notes

What about some other questions that might arise?

I want us to look briefly at some of the other questions that might come up for you at this time. Hopefully even a little guidance with these, will be helpful for you.

How do I manage all the visitors?

I remember talking to a neighbour, at the wake of another older neighbour, who had died. He mentioned to me how relieved he felt, that when he heard the news that the older man was poorly, he quickly called to the house. He did this, he told me, because he didn't want to turn up at the wake, not having visited his older neighbour in over a year!

When news has spread in their local community, that someone is very ill and likely approaching end of life, there can be a flurry of visitors. Many people want to come for the kindest and best-intentioned reasons. They want to show their regard for the person, or their support to the family. They want to make offers of help, or reassurances of prayerful remembrance. This can be a very comforting experience for the person, and for those close to them. It can however, also lead to a very busy household, and an already overwrought carer, having to try and find the time, or energy, to offer hospitality and to chat.

Some families have always had lots of visitors, other families, not so much. Some people thrive in the company and the distraction from caring, that the visitors provide. Other people find it exhausting. Some visitors are very sensitive to the needs of the person who is ill, and to those caring for them. They pre-arrange their visit, they stay only a short while, they decline any effortful hospitality, they offer practical as well as emotional support. Other people, for whatever reason, may not be so attuned. They might turn up, stay too long, and exhaust the person they have called to see, or their carer, or both. Even those who make short visits, may be unaware that lots of other people are also calling, even for short visits. All of these short visits can add up to a very full day.

There were times when I was working with people who had a palliative diagnosis, when I would visit their homes. I would meet the main carer, exhausted to the point of tears, who would point to a sittingroom in the house, filled with visitors entertaining themselves in each other's company. So many visitors, socialising with each other. Again, this isn't because they are unkind or uncaring, it may be that they just don't realise the unintended impact this could have, on the person, or on the family.

So, what might be helpful here. Well, think about what the person you are caring for is able for. If they feel able or keen for the visit, then that's great. If they don't feel able, you could act as a gatekeeper for that person. You could advise even well intentioned callers, that the person needs to rest, or isn't up to a visit. Or maybe you could let them know that you have things to do, and wouldn't be able to enjoy the visit at this time either. People who genuinely care for you and for the person, will understand and will not take any offence. They may even be able to offer to help with some of the things that need to be done.

If you are the one visiting, think about why you might want to be calling at this time. If you are a very close friend or family member, perhaps check with the main carer if it's a good time or day to visit. Perhaps you could help practically by bringing some tasty food for the main carer, or some treats or snacks to have with a cup of tea. Perhaps you could offer to mow the lawn, or pick up some groceries. Perhaps you could offer to help look after the person, and allow the main carer some time to take a break.

If you aren't a very close friend or relative, then perhaps this isn't the best time for you to be visiting. Perhaps the person or their family, need to have some time and space, to spend these days or hours by themselves. Perhaps think about some other ways you can show your care, support and concern? Maybe you can send a message to say you're thinking of the family. These thoughtful messages are likely to be warmly welcomed by the person, or their family or carers at this time.

Visitors can be a mixed blessing! So, if you are caring for someone who is approaching end of life, consider what is helpful for you at this time. Consider what might feel supportive, and what might feel more burdensome. This can be a lonely time for you. There may be one or two very close friends whose visits you would welcome. Many people do want to be supportive but aren't sure how to, and don't want to intrude. Maybe you could let them know you'd like them to call. If you keep the needs of the person you are caring for, and your needs, at the centre, you can make heartsome choices around visitors and visiting.

How do I try to take care of myself at this time?

Even thinking about this question, may cause you a bit of unease. Maybe you're wondering how on earth you could have time to think of yourself, in the midst of all that is needed, all that is going on around you. Maybe it feels a little selfish to you, to be thinking about yourself at such a time as this. I can understand that, but please let me gently assure you that this too, is an important question for you to consider here. It is not selfish at all, it is vital.

You are probably carrying a lot of responsibility at this time. You may be trying to manage a number of competing demands. You may not be getting as much sleep, or as much restful sleep, as you need. Perhaps your world has become much smaller, focused as it now is, on caring for this person who is approaching end of life. Perhaps you are carrying new worries, new and very mixed feelings. However wholehearted any of us are in our care and support, however grateful we feel that we are able to do it, it can be tiring, and can take a lot out of us.

And yes, this is a very different kind of time; it does ask so much more of us. And yes, we do recognise that the extra demands of this time, will pass. So, we keep turning up, as willing, generous carers, close family members or friends, to do what is needed. Alongside this, we do need to try and keep ourselves as healthy and well as we can, during this busier time.

At this time, you may not have the opportunity, or the energy, to do some of those things that usually restore you in mind and body. You may not, at the moment, have much time, or space, to meet with friends, go for a walk, read, watch a film. So, what might be possible for you? Are there some small things that would help lift your heart? Is there any scope for you to have an uninterrupted, quiet cup of tea? Could you get even a few minutes to walk outside and breathe fresh air? Could you take a little time to read and relish some of the messages sent to you by your close friends? Could you find a space to have a little time alone, to just sit, to steady yourself with some deep breaths, to listen to a favourite song, to say a prayer? Is there someone you could ask for help?

During these weeks and days and hours, it's probably more realistic for you to think about short, small, meaningful moments, that allow you to recover yourself. However small or short, these moments will help keep you well and sustain you in this difficult time. You too are worthy here, be gentle with yourself. Maybe think about what might be helpful, and manageable for you at this time, then give yourself permission to accept.

What do I say to the children?

This might be causing you some worry. You may yourself be trying to come to terms with all that's happening for you, or for you if you are the carer. You might be trying your best to manage your own heartache and fears and then work out whether or what to tell children. It might all feel very daunting for you, so let me reassure you, help is plentiful and available for you.

There is some wonderful and reliable information that hospice and palliative care charities have online. Both the Marie

Curie and Macmillan websites provide valuable guidance on speaking with children about serious illness, dying and death. There are also some beautiful little books, with stories written for children of different ages, about the dying and death of someone they love. Your local library might have some of these, and you could enquire there for some helpful titles. Your local specialist palliative team will also likely have some booklets or books that they can give you. So, daunting as this may feel, you are not alone, and there are many sources of good information and support to guide you.

To help you now, the heart of your response, could be shaped by this, whether you are telling children about your own serious illness and approaching death, or if you are the one caring for the person. Honesty here, works just as well for children as it does for you. Children may already have a sense something is wrong, may already be worrying. They may be fearing they have done something wrong. So, offering them age appropriate, gently paced, and accurate information, can be very reassuring for them. Coming from you, this will help them understand what is happening and allay some of their fears. Telling a child that nothing is wrong when they sense that there is something wrong is not helpful. These are hard conversations, so it is alright to let your children know that you are feeling sad too.

Clear, simple information is also good. For example, try not to say something like "granda has gone to sleep". For your child, going to sleep might become really scary, since, in their mind, granda went to sleep and never wakened up again. It's alright to say that the person has died, then allow the child to ask you any questions they have about this. Two of my favourite little books, that help small children grasp some understanding of dying and death, are, 'Waterbugs and Dragonflies' by Doris Stickney, and 'Badger's Parting Gifts', by Susan Varley. Both of these little books have been around a long time, but their messages are still so valuable. They might even help you too!

If you felt able, you might like to think about creating little story books or memory boxes with the children. You could use some pictures and drawings and memories you shared. You may not feel you have the energy or heart for this, and that is alright too. If you did feel able, doing activities like these together, with the children, can help with your conversations with them too.

You know your children or grandchildren best. You know how to talk to them about important things, in a way that they can understand. It is better that this sad news comes from you, or someone close to you, whom they can trust and who loves them. Having had this conversation with you, they can always come back to you, at a later time, if they have more questions or when they need some comforting. Trust yourself on this, and if you do feel you would like some more information, take a look at the resources list.

What happens now? When the person you cared for has died

Oh, I'm sure the very thought of this is painful for you; I am so sorry. In the midst of your heartache, your shock, your relief that the person who has died is now at peace, your grief, there are some practical things that do need to be attended to. But first, please allow yourself a little bit of time, to sit quietly with the person who has died, if that is something you would like to do. Allow yourself to connect in some way, with those very close to you, whether in person, or through a few messages, so that they can support you. Maybe they can help you contact others and let them know this sad news. Whatever it is you feel you need to do at this moment, allow yourself a little time.

If the person you were caring for died in hospital or a care home, then the staff will be able to guide you on what needs to happen now. If you were caring for the person at home, then here are a few of the practical tasks that need to be attended to. Maybe someone close to you, can help with these.

You will need to contact the person's GP, and let them know that the person has died. The GP will visit and do a final medical check to confirm and verify the death. This is a necessary task that allows you receive a death certificate for the person.

You will also need to contact an undertaker. Where I come from, the undertaker is well known in the person's local community. An experienced and professional undertaker will be a great source of guidance and support to you at this time. They will provide advice on each step to be taken over these next few days; the wake, the funeral and the burial.

You may have other norms and rituals, particular to your culture, which are followed at this time. Perhaps your priest, minister, or a spiritual advisor from your culture, will be able to guide you here. They may also be able to help you prepare a funeral liturgy, if the person who has died, hasn't already done so themselves.

Usually a few days following the funeral, another practical task that needs to be done at this time, is to contact the registrar's office, to register the death of the person you were caring for. This is usually within a few days of the death. Again, the undertaker is well placed to be able to advise on the specified time required for this, where you live.

If the person you cared for had a pension or received any other types of benefits payments, then you will need to notify those agencies too, that the person has died. You could contact your GP and ask them for the telephone number of the bereavement service in the province or country where you live. Usually, when you ring this number, they will take the details from you, of the person who has died. They will then, notify all of the relevant benefits agencies, on your behalf. This is a great service, and lessens the number of these types of phonecalls that you have to make, and the number of times you have to tell your sad news about the person's death. Often, these call handlers will have received bereavement training. They will, most likely, respond to you when you call, with great sensitivity and compassion. They will recognise and acknowledge, that this is a difficult and sad time. I know from my own experience, how kind and sensitive these call handlers have been.

I am so conscious, as I write, of how cold and business like all of this may read and sound to you. I'm sorry that it may come across as quite stark. I'm also conscious that if you are looking for this information, at this time, then you need it in a quick and easy to access way.

I also want to say to you, that of course, these immediate, practical tasks, are only a very small part of a much bigger, "what happens now" question. Considering this bigger question, brings you onwards into, what is likely to be, another unfamiliar, sometimes very painful place, where you touch into your own grief and loss.

Thankfully, there are many sources of support, information and guidance on bereavement services, which you can access and peruse, when you feel ready. There are wonderful resources on websites such as Bereaved NI, Children's Grief Centre, and Irish Hospice Foundation. These provide a wealth of easy to access, reliable information and support. There are also likely to be more local sources of bereavement support available for you. Perhaps your local health centre, or a local community or voluntary organisation, could give you some information on what's available near where you live. When you're ready, you have some idea about where to go for support.

But first, for now, maybe you just need to take a breath, have a rest, and try to slow down, even just a little. This has been a very sad and difficult time for you. You will need a little time to recover yourself. Sometimes, it's more than enough for now, to simply be where you are, and allow yourself a little bit time, before turning your attention to the next thing.

My own notes

Reflection: What about some other questions that might arise?

I stopped to watch the rain today.

I let the rhythm of its teeming, drench me through.

Soaking in, it cooled and stilled my haste.

That was all.

No, to gather breath, that is all.

So, I sat and watched the rain today.

If you would like to hear the reflection scan the QR code

My own notes

Postscript

So, how are you now? I imagine reading or listening to some of the content of this book, hasn't been that easy for you. You have done so well in staying with it. I felt writing some of it very hard too. Some of it reminded me of my own experience when I was standing where you are now. It can feel a very lonely place to stand, can't it? Often as I wrote, I thought of you, and wondered how you were getting on. These pages have marked something of the long and painful journey that all of us will travel, and explored some of the questions many of us might ask along the way.

We have tried to think through some of the big questions that arise for us when facing our own mortality, or when facing the end of life of someone we love or care for. We have tried to find some answers. More often, when the answers aren't so clear cut, we have tried to find the way that's best for us. We have come to understand, there isn't always a right or wrong; a should or shouldn't; a yes or no; so we look instead at what might be most helpful or useful, and do our best with that. I do hope there has been something of value for you here, and that you didn't feel quite so alone.

I am sure you have other questions that we haven't looked at in this book. Perhaps you have questions related to your experience or your particular circumstance, that we didn't fully explore together here. I do still hope that there was something within these pages, that offered you some light in response. Maybe think about who else might be able to help you with those questions. Is your local health centre a possible resource for you? Or a health and social care provider, a social worker, for example, whom you could approach for some advice? Maybe there's a local community or voluntary organisation which could help? Maybe a priest or minister could suggest where you could look for further information? Or maybe a close friend whom you trust?

There are some other sources of help and support available too. Reliable information is available online from some of the main hospice and palliative care websites, for example, Marie Curie, Macmillan, Hospice UK, Irish Hospice Foundation. Their work includes, among other things, treating and supporting people who are facing end of life, and supporting their families. These organisations have a wealth of experience, knowledge, and resources, which you might like to explore and find helpful. So, please don't ever feel you are alone, or have nowhere to turn.

For you and me, we come to the end of this book together. Let me say thank you to you. Thank you for allowing me to accompany you during some of this time. Through your reading or listening to this book, thank you for allowing me step into your life, your home and heart, in these weeks and days and hours. I hope my presence to you in these pages, has offered some small comfort, or given a little ease to you. Painful as this journeying time has been for you, I am grateful, that through this book, you allowed me walk alongside, some of the way.

As you step on from here, may you be blest with loving companions, gentle friends, and moments of solace and rest. May you be graced with a quiet presence to yourself, that serves your needs, and, at this time when there are few words, speaks to your heart. For now, go gently, go very, very gently.

My own notes

I've come to learn a little of how pliable is hope.
The way it flexes as it meets each shifting goal.
How it moves with freedom. With confidence to stretch
and so include what now has come to light.
It seems to yield the tired limits of any former prayer;
expanding, ever deepening in trust.
I see the bend and bow it makes, in widening its tent,
to give a place to changing circumstance.
And yet, in essence, stays the same, sure in its desire,
that what it's set its heart on here, is worthy.
It holds faithful to its promise, that when a time has come,
Hope will shift its shape again, to become the grace we
need.

If you would like to hear the
reflection scan the QR code

My own notes

148

A note from the publisher: Siobhan Maclean

I first met Deirdre only a few years ago. I have written a number of books for social workers, and Deirdre knew of some of those books. When I first moved to Northern Ireland, she reached out and generously invited me to her home. Deirdre has always given me a great sense of belonging and so when we talked about writing it was interesting that Deirdre felt she didn't 'belong' in that world. Thankfully, on reflection, Deirdre did decide to work on this book. Before I even saw the book, I said that I wanted to publish it. I had such confidence in what Deirdre would produce. I have seen the book in its various stages, but never have I seen such a complete text develop so quickly.

I have read the book a number of times as it has developed. It has struck me in different ways at different times and each time I have read it I have taken something different from it. I am very fortunate that I still have both my parents, but I am at the age where I have started to worry about them, and I have become more and more aware of their ageing over the last few years. This book has really helped me to take some time to think about the questions that I have, even though there are no specific concerns about their lives at this time. The book has given me the courage to think about things and to have some very beginning conversations with my parents and my adult daughters about dying and death.

I have tried to act as a 'critical friend' to Deirdre as she has written this book asking questions and offering my own reflections as the book has grown. Towards the end of the process, we have reflected together on the title 'When there are few words.' In fact, there are more than 25,000 words in this book, but those words come from a place of experience, of humility, of generosity and we decided that the title was fitting because generally people do not have words. How many times have I not known what to say to friends when they have experienced a loss? Reading this book has not only helped me to explore my own thoughts about how to best navigate the dying and death that will become a part of my life, but it has also helped me to find the words to talk to my friends about their own losses. We hope that this book will help you to find your own words as you navigate this issue as a natural part of life.

I have no experience of audiobooks, but we decided that this book should also be available in audio form. There have been stages as this book has developed that Deirdre has read some of the text to me and as I have heard it, I have seen it differently than when I read it. Reading and listening are clearly different experiences. We wanted this opportunity to be available to everyone and so together we learnt a little more about audiobooks. As I write this, I am hopeful that we will be able to follow up with an audiobook version.

In my career I have talked a lot about the importance of kindness and working from the heart. I have always said that things can be nice, but only people can be kind. My work with Deirdre on this book has changed my view on that. This book is kind. There is little more to say than that. This is a beautiful book that offers kindness at a point in life where nothing is really more important to the reader.

Other sources of information you may like to explore...

Please note that different countries will have different policies and legislation, so do check what is applicable where you live.

Dr Kathryn Mannix' short video
https://www.bbc.co.uk/ideas/videos/dying-is-not-as-bad-as-you-think/p062m0xt

Advance Care Planning	https://www.health-ni.gov.uk/advance- care-planning-now-and-future
Resuscitation Council UK	https://www.resus.org.uk
Marie Curie	https://www.mariecurie.org.uk
Macmillan	https://www.macmillan.org.uk
All Ireland Institute of hospice and palliative care	https://aiihpc.org
Compassionate Communities NI	https://compassionatecommunitiesni.com
Community Developement and Health Network	https://www.cdhn.org
NISCC Learning Zone	https://learningzone.niscc.info/learning-resources-main/
Cancer Fund for Children	https://cancerfundforchildren.com/

Waterbugs and Dragonflies by Doris Stickney

Badger's Parting Gifts by Susan Varley

Grief And Bereavement

https://bereaved.hscni.net/

https://www.childrensgriefcentre.ie/

https://hospicefoundation.ie/

Scotland	https://ihub.scot/improvement-programmes/community-care/palliative-and-end-of-life-care-1/
Canada	https://www.canada.ca/en/health-canada/services/health-services-benefits/palliative-care.html
New Zealand	https://www.tewhatuora.govt.nz/for-health-professionals/clinical-guidance/specific-life-stage-health-information/palliative/
Australia	https://palliativecare.org.au/resource/what-is-palliative-care/